Here is a book for the busy practitioner and others, which is rigorous, relevant and readable. Full of easy to assimilate, well-expressed argument and poignant examples it has a practical immediacy which keeps the pages turning. It covers an important issue for everyone committed to effective and well-informed social care practice and policy, which is a professional responsibility for all social workers.

Dr Ray Jones, Director of Adult and Community Services, Wiltshire County Council

A mine of much-needed, well-written help for those who want to use research evidence to improve outcomes for service users. For reading from front to back, or for dipping into; for all social workers -whether you want to 'get going' or refine your understanding and skills.

Celia Atherton, Director, Research in Practice, Dartington

I think the major strength of this account of evidence-based policy and practice is its common sense, plain speaking style, well suited to a topic that is often drowned in jargon. It speaks the language of its policy and practice audience, includes examples with direct practice relevance, and helps readers to direct their own learning about the demands of evidence-based policy and practice. For the teacher of evidence-based policy and practice, and for researchers, there is a welcome emphasis on the value of different kinds of evidence, on the detail of locating and analysing studies, and on the contribution of service users and carers to creating knowledge; the account avoids polarising qualitative and quantitative approaches to knowledge; and a final strength is the attention given to staying research-minded.

In short, this is an intelligent and reflective book that makes a major contribution to demystifying evidence-based policy and practice.

Professor Mike Fisher AcSS, Director of Research & Reviews, Social Care Institute for Excellence (SCIE)

This is a seriously important book. As government commissions more systematic literature reviews on best-value cost effective interventions; as centres around the country are developing information webpages on 'what works'; as courses are being set up to teach Evidence Based Social Work; as social workers are asked to undertake interventions with their clients that are likely to be effective; as social projects will only get funded if they can demonstrate that what they plan to do is likely to promote better outcomes for their customers, the signs are clear. Woolly ideology in the caring professions that well-meaning people must be making a difference as long as they care, is not good enough. Those in need have a right to know that the help they receive is more likely to help their problem rather than harm, and government and others will only pay for interventions that are likely to make a positive difference.

But what actually is evidence based social work? This book is right to identify that the new movement is perplexing. Written in an easy-to-read style this book makes the inaccessible, accessible. How do you find the evidence, what matters and what doesn't? With the many research findings how do you sort the wheat from the chaff? How do you make sense of the statistics. The answers are all in this excellent book. We will use it on our course: MSc in Evidence Based Social Work. I strongly recommend it.

Dr Ann Buchanan, Director of Oxford Centre for Research in Parenting and Children, and University Reader in Social Work, Oxford

Evidence-Based Social Work

A Guide for the Perplexed

**Tony Newman, Alice Moseley
Stephanie Tierney and Annemarie Ellis**

Russell House Publishing

First published in 2005 by:
Russell House Publishing Ltd.
4 St. George's House
Uplyme Road
Lyme Regis
Dorset DT7 3LS

Tel: 01297-443948
Fax: 01297-442722
e-mail: help@russellhouse.co.uk
www.russellhouse.co.uk

British Library Cataloguing-in-publication Data:

A catalogue record for this book is available from the British Library.

ISBN: 1-903855-55-1

Typeset by TW Typesetting, Plymouth, Devon
Printed by Antony Rowe, Chippenham

About Russell House Publishing

RHP is a group of social work, probation, education and youth and
community work practitioners and academics working in
collaboration with a professional publishing team.
Our aim is to work closely with the field to produce innovative
and valuable materials to help managers, trainers, practitioners
and students.
We are keen to receive feedback on publications and new ideas for
future projects.
For details of our other publications please visit our website or ask
us for a catalogue. Contact details are on this page.

Contents

Foreword

International studies of the effectiveness of social work interventions, from the 1970s onwards, have been telling us roughly the same things. However, there is one particularly robust set of findings at the head of the list. As in the literature of the other helping professions, we routinely underestimate the gap between acquiring knowledge and putting this knowledge into practice, especially when staff, or organisations, are under stress. Indeed there is a paradox that always emerges on training courses on evidence-based practice. Although social workers are enthusiastic about the idea, they often feel powerless to act in their workplace settings.

Now we have a book, which not only explains evidence-based social work, but illustrates its importance in improving outcomes for those with whom we work. It is concise, practical, literate, and scientifically robust in the evidence it draws upon. Also, it is written by people who have got their hands dirty in taking the key messages and skills to the front line and into management meetings. Above all, this is as much a 'how to' book as a 'why don't we...?' text. The authors' achievement is to have combined the best, that is, the most bias-reducing research with a detailed knowledge of the demanding challenges of day-to-day practice. We hope that practitioners and students will snap it up.

Professor Brian Sheldon, former Director of the Centre for Evidence-Based Social Services, University of Exeter and **Dr Chris Hanvey**, Barnardo's UK Director of Operations.

About the authors

All the authors are actively involved in working with practitioners, managers, service users, research institutes and the broader academic community to bridge the gap between research and practice.

Tony Newman is Principal Research Officer with Barnardo's. He previously worked as a social worker in the USA and UK, and subsequently as a manager of community-based learning disability services in South Wales. He is author of *What Works in Building Resilience?* (Barnardo's, 2004) and *Children of Disabled Parents* (RHP, 2003), co-author of *What Works for Parents with Learning Disabilities?* (Barnardo's, 2005) and co-editor of *What Works for Children?* (Open University Press, 2002), and has published numerous articles and reports. His main research interests are the impact of parental disability on children, the promotion of resilience and the implementation of evidence-based practice.

Alice Moseley was a researcher at the Centre for Evidence-Based Social Services (CEBSS) and is now a PhD student at the University of Exeter. She has been involved in the development of training and resources to promote and support evidence-based practice among frontline social care staff throughout the South West of England. Her specialist areas of work include the dissemination of research to practitioners, particularly through electronic media, and developing evidence-based organisational cultures. Her research interests include inter-agency working and the role of research evidence in the policy process.

Stephanie Tierney has worked as a researcher at CEBSS for over three years, during which time she has played a role in the development and delivery of training in critical appraisal skills and accessing research via the internet. She has also been involved in a large survey which looked at the views and knowledge of social care practitioners towards evidence-based practice. She has recently completed a PhD on the theme of adolescents with anorexia nervosa.

Annemarie Ellis is a Research Fellow at CEBSS, and a Research Facilitator for Mid Devon Primary Care Research Group. She has over 10 years experience of conducting research in social care and health fields. She has taught critical appraisal skills and research methods to health care staff and, in the last two years, guided the development of CEBSS' critical appraisal skills programme. She has strong interests in social care and health services for older people; user involvement in research; and developing research methodologies which are practical, valid and reliable.

Acknowledgements

The content of this book is based on our own experience, but also that of numerous colleagues past and present, especially at Barnardo's and the Centre for Evidence-Based Social Services, on whose knowledge we have drawn and in some cases, shamelessly plundered.

We would especially like to thank Dr Sara Scott of Barnardo's, and Professor Brian Sheldon and David Hess of CEBSS for their comments on early drafts of the book.

We are also very grateful to Stewart Macwilliam and Peter Maggs, librarians at the Universities of Exeter and Newcastle respectively, and Christopher Reeve, Barnardo's librarian, for their advice and help on Chapter 2.

A particular debt of gratitude is owed to the many practitioners, especially from the CEBSS member authorities and Barnardo's, whose experience and insights have informed this book.

The views expressed within however, and any errors or omissions, are the sole responsibility of the authors.

Introduction

Recall the face of the poorest person you may have seen and ask yourself if the step you contemplate is of any use to them.

(M.K. Gandhi)

What is this book about?

This book is primarily concerned with the evidence base of social work and social care practice. More precisely, our focus is on the *application* of this evidence base. The aim is to help the reader understand the principles of evidence-based practice, learn some associated skills, and apply these skills to their work.

In an increasingly information-rich environment we all – as professionals, users of social care services, National Health Service patients or just plain citizens – need a variety of skills to evaluate the often conflicting messages with which we are bombarded on a daily basis. Anyone today with use of a personal computer and a modem – predicted to be one billion of us by 2005 – is exposed to more information than any person in history who lived prior to the development of the World Wide Web. However, merely having access to knowledge is of little use without the capacity to sift it for relevance, accuracy and usefulness. The days are long gone when certain types of knowledge were available only to a limited number of specialists. One consequence of the information revolution is the increasingly public debate on the effectiveness – or ineffectiveness – of activities undertaken by social care, education, para-medical and health services. Much of this debate is driven by the conclusions of research studies. Take the claims and counter-claims that the ordinary reader of a newspaper has to make sense of over their breakfast on any Sunday of the month. On 22 February 2004, we were told that:

The Department of Health is spending millions of pounds on public health campaigns without any evidence that they actually work, an official report will conclude this week . . . Mr Wanless singles out for particular criticism the provision of NHS clinics to help smokers quit. He points out that ministers have no evidence they are effective.

(*Independent on Sunday*)

Tracey is one of the success stories of a nationwide drive to teach the parents of children with serious behavioural problems how to do a better job of raising their offspring . . . research carried out on the work shows that although only just over a half of all parenting orders are completed, offending behaviour is reduced by a third as a result.

(Observer)

Andrew Wakefield . . . identified a new inflammatory bowel disorder linked to autism . . . autism had appeared after the triple MMR (measles mumps and rubella) vaccination . . . Andrew Wakefield urged parents to give their children single vaccines at annual intervals, whereas Professor Arie Zuckerman, a virologist and dean of the medical school, insisted MMR had been given to millions of children around the world and was safe . . . in the six years since, national vaccination rates against MMR have fallen from above 90 per cent to below 80 per cent, dropping so low in some areas that measles outbreaks are threatened.

(Independent on Sunday)

The Airborne Initiative is a unique project which puts 18–25 year old persistent offenders through a gruelling nine week programme that includes tough outdoor physical activities . . . research carried out by Stirling University suggests that Airborne cuts reconviction rates by 21 per cent but last week the Scottish Executive decided to withdraw the project's funding claiming it was not effective enough . . . 'it wasn't getting the number of referrals it was funded for and the drop out rate was too high. It's more expensive than an equivalent time in prison'.

(Independent on Sunday)

These issues pose dilemmas for us as citizens, practitioners and policy makers. As citizens, should we, if we wish to quit smoking, now find another solution rather than an NHS clinic? If we are experiencing difficulties with the behaviour of our young children, is a parenting programme the answer? Our baby is due for her MMR inoculation but we are worried about the alleged link with autism – whom do we believe? Our eldest son is a persistent offender and half way through the Airborne programme – should we lobby the Scottish Executive to prevent its closure? And where do we stand as professionals? In addition to our practice and personal experience, what additional information do we need – and where do we find it – in order to offer sound advice to vulnerable and often confused people? As social care managers, in which strategies do we choose to place our limited resources? As policy makers, on what sources of evidence do we rely when making investment decisions that can affect the lives of thousands of people? Whether we are choosing a procedure for ourselves or recommending one for others, we want the maximum level of assurance that it will be effective, have no unwanted side effects, will be better than competing procedures that we might have chosen, and certainly be better than doing nothing. The purpose of evidence-based practice in social care is to find ways of making this level of assurance as strong as possible, both for ourselves and our loved ones, as well as people we serve in a professional capacity.

The 'evidence' we need to make sound decisions about people's welfare derives from professional experience, the views and preferences of service users, and the knowledge found in any profession's research literature. These are the three key elements that comprise the evidence base of social work and social care practice. Historically, social care staff have been strong on the first element, are increasingly good on the second, and rather poor on the third. 'Research' differs from other methods of knowledge acquisition in a number of important ways. It is an activity characterised by a systematic approach to conducting an enquiry. It should be *transparent*, in that we are able to understand why and how the inquiry was conducted, and, *objective*, the best test of which is generally the reporting of results the authors would prefer not to have found. It should also – for our purposes in this book – have *utility*, that is, have some practical relevance to the circumstances of social care service users. Lastly, a profession's research base must be *incremental*, that is, should consciously build on previous achievements. Such developments are not always linear, and many findings are highly resilient to the march of time. Overall, however, we would all rather be served by professionals whose knowledge base has been reliably built and continually updated, and who will adjust their practice accordingly as new and trustworthy information emerges.

Sound professional decision making requires a mastery of the whole evidential universe, not just part of it. As well as drawing on practice experience and listening carefully to the views of service users, we need to understand what research evidence is, why it is important, where to find it, how to appraise it and how to apply it in situations commonly encountered by social care professionals. This book describes the core skills required.

Who is this book for?

This book is aimed at both professional social workers and the broader social care workforce. Many of the procedures and principles discussed will also be of relevance to allied professions. As the title of the book implies, you are about to enter a resource aimed not only at explaining the *what* of evidence-based practice, or the *why*, but also the *how*. Having read it, you should be clearer about what evidence-based practice is, why it is essential to effective and ethical social care practice, and how you can carry it out on a day to day basis. We hope that this book will not only help you develop an evidence-based dimension to your practice, but also stimulate your enthusiasm to search for new knowledge and ideas.

Structure of the book

The book begins by describing what evidence-based practice (EBP) is and what it isn't, why some kinds of information are more important and reliable than others, and how evidence-based practice can contribute to better outcomes for service users. Chapter 2 and 3 discuss how to ask questions, how to locate relevant research information, especially from on-line sources, and how to critically appraise the material found. A modest level of competence in statistical techniques – or at least an understanding of their importance – is a valuable asset for any practitioner. Chapter 4 provides a gentle introduction to the more important techniques. Service users are central to our mission. Chapter 5 describes how service users can become directly involved in research production themselves, and how we can develop information that can help people make informed choices about the services offered to them. Chapter 6 discusses how we can embed evidence-based practice into our day to day work. The book concludes with an extensive resources section which flags up the most important sources of research information and guidance on evidence-based practice. We have refrained from including detailed search guides to the more well-known open access databases, as any advice given may become obsolete by the time of this book's publication. Readers are strongly advised to use the on-line search engines of the respective databases, which are normally very easy to follow, and have the advantage over the printed page of always being up to date. Resources are organised around the six core chapters of the book, using the symbols below:

Introducing EBP   *Accessing research*

Appraising research   *Understanding statistics*

User involvement   *Implementation*

Evidence, schmevidence . . .

We would be the first to concede that the term evidence-based practice has some image problems within social work. Rightly or wrongly, it has become associated with approaches which elevate empirical and quantitative sources of knowledge to a pinnacle of authority, diminish the value of practitioner experience, intuition and insight, underestimate the complexity of human affairs and fail to acknowledge the importance of context and process [1]. As a result, a number of alternatives have been suggested, including 'knowledge-based practice' [2] and 'evidence-informed practice' [3]. These suggestions are based on a similar concern; to express better the blend of research evidence, practice knowledge and user experience that should drive decision making in social care. While recognising the issues associated with this search for alternative descriptions, we prefer to retain the term 'evidence-based practice' for a number of reasons. First, international professions, of which social work is one, need a common language (not least for locating research evidence through the use of standardised search terms, of which more later) and having competing terms to describe the same phenomenon is at best unhelpful, and at worst downright confusing. Furthermore, inter-disciplinary work is an essential feature of social care practice. A common language is necessary for effective communication between professions as well as within a single profession; evidence-based practice is a term widely used within medicine, mental health services, education, psychology and nursing. There are enough linguistic barriers to effective inter-agency working already; we don't need to erect more. Second, there are opportunity costs involved in generating and promoting alternative and competing descriptions, and we believe that the time is better spent on practical issues rather than discussions on terminology. Third, 'evidence' is, according to the Oxford English Dictionary, 'information, whether in the form of personal testimony, the language of documents, or the production of material objects', a definition elastic enough to more than encompass the sources of knowledge that all agree are essential to effective practice. We have therefore chosen to invest our energy in describing what evidence-based practice is, and how to practice it, rather than what it should be called.

We have also not sought to describe in any depth the genesis of evidence-based practice in health care services [4–6], the critiques that have challenged the application of the paradigm in medicine [7], psychology [8] and social work [9–11], the counter-arguments [12–14], or the recent debate on the ways in which we can classify different kinds of knowledge [15]. These have been discussed at considerable length, and the interested reader can consult them should they wish.

. . . and other terminological disputes

We have titled this book 'Evidence-Based Social Work', rather than 'social care' as we strongly believe that the skills associated with evidence-based practice are an inseparable part of the professional social worker's knowledge base. This by no means implies that the broader social care workforce should not seek to practice in an 'evidence-based' way. Rather, it is in recognition that a claim to professional status carries obligations, not least of which is establishing and maintaining public confidence, and this must be fulfilled by continual learning and the application of new concepts and ideas from research. We do not share the view, depressingly persistent in some circles, that professionalism and ethical practice are inversely related [16]; rather, we would argue that authority and autonomy – the essential corollaries of professional status – are essential for client empowerment and service accountability [17]. We believe benefits will accrue to both social workers and those they serve when these privileges are justifiably earned. Where appropriate we also, somewhat unfashionably, use the term 'client' alongside the more common 'service user', to stress the professional obligations of social care staff. We also, to avoid confusion, continue to use the term 'social services department' to describe the unit of local government responsible for the statutory delivery of social care services, rather than the more accurate, but less familiar, Council with Social Service Responsibilities (CSSR).

One *mea culpa* should be acknowledged by those of us who have been working to promote evidence-based practice in social care. We especially deplore the tendency – regrettably not entirely absent from some studies cited otherwise approvingly in this book – to describe research evidence as if it were a product solely aimed at improving decision making by professionals, rather than also stressing its function as an aid to help people who depend on social care services make decisions about what is best for them. It has been argued that the biggest impact of evidence-based practice on medicine will be a restructuring of doctor-patient relationships as more patient-focused information on effective procedures becomes available, and patients are able to play, should they wish, a more active role in decision making [18]. The 'informed' patient is rapidly becoming a reality. We are some way off having a similarly informed 'client' population and are unlikely, given the mixture of elective and coercive services typical of social care, to go as far down this path as we might in our role as NHS patients. However, a knowledgeable client is an empowered client. The quality and effectiveness of our social welfare interventions will improve when those on the receiving end are able to influence its delivery by complementing their personal experiences with access to independent sources of information on programme effectiveness.

References

[1] Smith, D. (2000) The limits of positivism revisited. In seminar series: What works as evidence for practice? The methodological repertoire in an applied discipline (27 April 2000) at: http://www.elsc.org.uk/socialcareresource/tswr/seminar5/smith.htm

[2] Humphreys, C., Berridge, D., Butler, I. and Ruddick, R. (2003) Making research count: the development of 'knowledge-based practice'. *Research Policy and Planning.* 21: 1, 41–9.

[3] Hodson, R. and Cooke, E. (2004) Leading the drive for evidence-informed practice. *Journal of Integrated Care.* 12: 1, 12–8.

[4] Ramchandani, P., Joughin, C. and Zwi, M. (2001) Evidence-based child and adolescent mental health services: oxymoron or brave new dawn? *Child Psychology and Psychiatry Review.* 6: 2, 59–64.

[5] Muir Gray, J.A. (2001) *Evidence Based Healthcare: How to Make Health Policy and Management Decisions.* Edinburgh: Churchill Livingstone.

[6] Evans, D. and Haines, A. (Eds.) (2000) *Implementing Evidence-based Changes in Healthcare.* Abingdon: Radcliffe Medical Press.

[7] Williams, D. and Garner, J. (2002) The case against 'the evidence': a different perspective on evidence-based medicine. *British Journal of Psychiatry.* 180: 8–12.

[8] Larner, G. (2004) Family therapy and the politics of evidence. *Journal of Family Therapy.* 26: 17–39.

[9] Trinder, L. (1996) Social work research: the state of the art (or science). *Child and Family Social Work.* 1: 233–42.

[10] Witkin, S. (1999) Constructing our future. – editorial. *Social Work.* 44: 1, 5–8.

[11] Webb, S. (2001) Some considerations on the validity of evidence-based practice in social work. *British Journal of Social Work.* 31: 57–79.

[12] Sheldon, B. (2001) The validity of evidence-based practice in social work: a reply to Stephen Webb. *British Journal of Social Work.* 31: 801–9.

[13] Gibbs, L. and Gambrill, E. (2002) Evidence-based practice: counterarguments to objections. *Research on Social Work Practice.* 12: 3, 452–76.

[14] Munro, E. (1998) *Understanding Social Work: An Empirical Approach.* London: Athlone Press.

[15] Pawson, R., Boaz, A., Grayson, L., Long, A. and Barnes, C. (2003) *Types and Quality of Knowledge in Social Care. Knowledge Review No. 3.* London: Social Care Institute for Excellence.

[16] Bisman, C. (2004) Social work values: the moral code of the profession. *British Journal of Social Work.* 34: 109–23.

[17] Cooper, A., Hetherington, R. and Katz, I. (2003) *The Risk Factor: Making the Child Protection System Work for Children.* London: Demos.

[18] Coulter, A. (1999) Paternalism or partnership? Patients have grown up: and there is no going back. *British Medical Journal.* 319, 719–20.

Chapter 1

Introducing Evidence-based Practice

This chapter discusses:
- What evidence-based practice is (and isn't).
- Why it is important to practitioners.
- Why we must make judgements about the value of different kinds of evidence.
- How evidence-based practice can benefit service users.

You shall neither side with the mighty . . . nor shall you show deference to a poor man in his dispute.

(Exodus 23: 2–3)

Building a profession

Social work, at least in recent decades, has been less concerned than other professions with developing a research base for its activities. Social workers have rarely been expected to pay much attention to the literature underpinning their profession once their course of training has finished [1]. Where such interest does exist, social workers rightly complain that the essential features which mark a profession are frequently absent from their workplaces – libraries, dedicated study time, information technology, access to professional journals, national and international networks – and perhaps most importantly, a valuing of curiosity and knowledge seeking by employers. Inter-agency and multi-disciplinary work is now the rule rather than the exception in most areas of social care practice. This makes it all the more urgent that professionals are able to speak the same language, and communicate with each other using similar assumptions about the respective strengths and weaknesses of different types of professional knowledge [2]. Social work practice cannot afford to go its separate way. The obstacles are many, and will require considerable application of energy and resources to resolve.

Important building blocks, however, are increasingly falling into place. Social care practitioners are expected to base their work, like that of other professions, on evidence of 'what works' [3] and to 'take responsibility for maintaining and improving their knowledge and skills' [4]. A number of consortia, funded from a variety of local government, central government and voluntary sector sources, have begun to deliver training, material and support for evidence-based practice across all areas of social care:

- The Centre for Evidence-Based Social Services,[1] currently based at the University of Exeter, works with (at the time of writing) 20 local authorities across England.
- Research in Practice,[2] with bases in Dartington and Sheffield, focuses on work with children, and serves over 100 partners and members in the statutory and voluntary sectors.
- Making Research Count[3] is a university based collaboration between 10 colleges and some 40 member agencies.
- The Economic and Social Research Council (ESRC) has funded an evidence-based policy and practice initiative,[4] part of which focuses on reviews of effective interventions and implementation procedures in child care practice.[5]
- An international consortium, the Campbell Collaboration[6] has begun to construct a library of trials and systematic reviews of interventions in social care, education and criminology, based on a model already in existence for health care practice.
- A virtual learning resource to help social care practitioners become and stay 'research minded' is available from the University of Southampton.[7]
- The mission of the Social Care Institute for Excellence (SCIE), an independent body funded by the Department of Health and the Wales Assembly,[8] is to improve the quality of practice by collecting and disseminating knowledge to service users and the social care community.

Recent support from SCIE to the Centre for Evidence-Based Social Services, the University of Southampton and Research in Practice means that all the knowledge databases, training materials and other resources available from the above websites can now be accessed by anyone. These organisations, and others that will be described in this book, vary in their approach, but all have an important role in helping practitioners access, digest and utilise research

---

[1] *www.cebss.org*
[2] *www.rip.org.uk*
[3] *www.makingresearchcount.org.uk*
[4] *www.evidencenetwork.org*
[5] *www.whatworksforchildren.org.uk*
[6] *www.campbellcollaboration.org*
[7] *www.resmind.swap.ac.uk*
[8] *www.scie.org.uk*

findings. There are increasingly few excuses for practitioners not to be aware of the research literature underpinning their particular area of work and to keep up to date with new developments. One very good excuse, however, remains. Social work training has placed little emphasis on teaching practitioners how to formulate a research question relevant to their work, locate information that may help answer it, appraise the quality of the material found, and incorporate the findings into their practice [5]. These are not the only skills, and not always the most important, required by those working in the social care community. However, they are an essential part of any claim to professional status, and as such, form the heart of this book.

Process and outcomes

All of these recent initiatives share, to varying degrees, the belief that we are failing to utilise adequately the research knowledge that already exists. Primary research – that is the development of new studies – is undoubtedly important. Currently, however, the main task of the social care research community is to synthesise accurately what we know about the effectiveness of interventions, disseminate this knowledge to the social care profession, work with practitioners and managers to build on good practice and, where appropriate, effect change. By *effectiveness*, we mean the capacity of an intervention to deliver the outcomes specified in advance, that is, in the words of the famous advertising slogan, 'to do what it says on the tin'. Unlike too often in the past, academic research production is beginning to pay greater attention to the *outcome* of social care interventions, that is, the effect our work actually has on the people who rely on us. This is long overdue. While the ethical qualities of services have historically been stressed by both the British and American professional social work associations [6, 7], less effort has been devoted to examining their effectiveness [8]. Social work research in the UK, and indeed the USA, has consisted disproportionately of theoretical and descriptive studies. In the USA, studies which examine the effectiveness of social work interventions account for only 14 per cent of articles in social work journals [9]. The UK appears to do rather worse; of the 356 articles appearing in the *British Journal of Social Work* during the 1990s, only five were outcome studies [10]. Academic research in social work has remained curiously reluctant to meet the information needs of its core professional user group. This is not a satisfactory situation for a profession whose primary task is intervention and change, not observation and commentary.

Evidence-based practice – the what, the why and the how

As in other professions, it is important that professionally qualified social workers base their practice on the best evidence of what works for clients and are responsive to new ideas from research [11].

What is evidence-based practice?

The definition most frequently used to describe evidence-based practice is 'the *conscientious*, *explicit* and *judicious* use of current best evidence in making decisions about the care of individuals' [12]. What do we mean by these three elements?

Conscientious – governed by a sense of duty. Professionals should be equipped with the knowledge to justify their claims to special expertise. Knowledge, however, should not be a fixed and finite entity, acquired in training, and frozen upon receipt of certificate and graduation photograph. In order to discharge their obligations ethically, professionals must continue to learn, and adapt their practice accordingly. This adaptation must draw on sound up to date evidence of what appears to be effective, and ineffective, and even more importantly, what appears to do harm.

Explicit – distinctly expressing all that is meant. Service providers proposing to use or commission a particular service or intervention should be able to make clear on what basis the choice was made. Explicitness involves the consideration of different options with clients, based on a review of what is known about the most effective ways of helping people in situations such as theirs, with the aim of building a collaborative and informed relationship. People who use services, and those who invest in and manage them, need to have a shared understanding of why services of a particular type and structure are being delivered. In other words, the 'workings-out' that underpin the rationale for a service need to be made clear.

Judicious – exercising sound judgement. While practitioners should, in order to practice in an evidence-based way, have a detailed knowledge of the relevant research base, professional judgement can never rest on this dimension alone. Research evidence is usually based on the aggregated experiences or views of large numbers – sometimes many thousands – of people. Just as the laws which govern the behaviour of gases fail when applied to single molecules, so findings from research – even the most robust and valid ones – can only be applied with confidence to these large populations, not necessarily to each and every one of the people who make up the population [13]. Decision making at an individual level must also be informed by professional judgement, intuition and an intimate knowledge of the client's personal narrative. Judicious decision making will require all these elements to be taken into account.

A greater stress on *effectiveness* and other concepts associated with evidence-based practice has increasingly penetrated the social care universe over the past decade. For example, CareData, which is maintained by the Social Care Institute for Excellence, is the largest UK database for abstracts of books, journals and other material relevant to social care. Over the past decade, the percentage of abstracts containing the keyword 'outcomes' has increased tenfold. In the same period, the number of indexed abstracts which contain the term 'evidence-based practice' has increased from zero to over 100 per year, as illustrated below.

Table 1.1 CareData abstracts containing the term 'evidence-based practice' 1993–2003 (search conducted 21/12/04 *www.scie.org.uk*)

1993	1994	1995	1996	1997	1998	1999	2000	2001	2002	2003	Total 1993–2003
0	1	1	3	14	24	80	107	93	129	139	591

It is, of course, the ideas underpinning evidence-based practice not the term itself which is of significance, so it is important that we dispose of a persistent misunderstanding at the outset. Contrary to popular belief, evidence-based practice is not about searching for a 'right' answer, because there is rarely one 'right' answer to any of the problems that social workers face – though service users can reasonably expect some consistency in responses when the same question is asked of different professionals.[9] It is better conceived of as a strategy which aims to maximise the odds in favour of a client. Evidence-based practice cannot deliver certainties, just increase probabilities, and this is the most that any approach claiming to be 'evidence-based' can hope to achieve. The task is to be fully appraised of the available options, and to choose the one – wherever possible in consultation with service users – that is most likely to lead to a good outcome. A detailed and up to date knowledge of available options, their respective desirability given the particular circumstances of the client, a degree of expertise greater than that of the lay public, and the capacity to offer clear advice untainted by covert influence from special interest groups is, we would suggest, what the public expects of any profession. At some time in our lives most of us will

---

[9] Diagnostic agreement is measured by the κ (kappa) score, where 0.1 represents a very low, and 1.0 a perfect degree of consensus. This is discussed more fully in Chapter 4.

crossover – if we have not already – from being professionals to becoming service users, and we will expect any assistance we receive to be supported by a robust evidence base as to its effectiveness, rather than it being provided simply because it is in fashion, or reflects the preferences, theories, political or personal beliefs of the provider. If we have to depend on social care or health professionals, we expect the advice given to be authoritative, but not authoritarian [14]. For example, assessment has long been recognised as an essential social work skill. Many, perhaps most of us, will be subject to some kind of assessment on our journey from the cradle to the grave, whether for an entitlement, to examine our capacity to perform certain tasks, to ascertain our vulnerability, or to establish our need for a service. Social workers who undertake assessments are expected to draw substantially on knowledge which combines a detailed understanding of the instrument used, an acquaintance with the specific circumstances of the respective client group including cultural sensitivity, skills in interviewing, familiarity with the research base and a capacity for critical thinking [15]. Service users have a right to expect any social worker to use the most appropriate instrument for the job, to know about the merits and demerits of possible competitors, to possess the required interpersonal and technical skills, and have the necessary authority to complete the task. Carers have clearly expressed a preference for social workers with autonomy and decision making capacity, rather than functionaries who continually need to seek permission from others over resource allocation [16].

Why is evidence-based practice important?

Contemporary interest in providing effective services has a long and impressive lineage. Joseph Rowntree, at the end of the nineteenth century, and Mary Richmond, writing at the beginning of the twentieth, were both concerned about the effectiveness of public welfare services. The latter remarked:

> We should welcome, therefore, the evident desire of social workers to abandon claims to respect based on good intentions alone; we should meet halfway their earnest endeavours to subject the processes of their task to critical analysis; and should encourage them to measure their work by the best standards being applied by experience [17].

Indeed, during this period, the effectiveness – especially the cost effectiveness – of welfare services was a preoccupation of the regulatory authorities, the Poor Law unions and the large philanthropic organisations. Speaking to an audience of social scientists in 1879, Thomas Barnardo, who had founded the Barnardo's organisation just over a decade earlier, provided an early example of a cost benefit analysis. A choice needed to be made, he suggested, between expenditure:

. . . in the shape of rates and taxes for the support of police, magistrates, justices, houses of detention, convict prisons . . . or in the form of donations to institutions like ours . . . every convict costs England upwards of £80 per head per annum. Every boy or girl taken from the streets costs but £16 per year [18].[10]

Thus, while the phrase 'evidence-based practice' may be modern, the principles behind it are not; they have simply been rejuvenated in recent decades, most forcefully in medicine, but increasingly in other professions, including psychology, psychiatry, psychotherapy, criminology and education. Indeed, the influential 1972 monograph often cited as the midwife of evidence-based medicine also considered, albeit briefly, the application of evidence-based practice to social work. As well as being free at the point of delivery, it was argued that 'care', whether medical or social, should also be *effective*. While expressing concern about the inflationary effects of infinite demand and limited supply in the NHS, a warning was also flagged up to the newly created local authority social services departments:

. . . the Social Services seem to be evolving exactly in the same unfortunate way as medicine by suggesting that wherever there is a social 'need' a social worker must be appointed whether or not there is any evidence that the social worker can alter the natural history of the social problem [19].

Indignation at inequality and oppression is an indispensable part of the social work mission; however, indignation serves little useful purpose when it is de-coupled from a careful consideration of whether our resulting activities actually help anyone.

Evidence-based practice calls for decision making that is considered rather than reactive. All interventions – social as well as pharmacological and surgical – have the capacity to cause harm as well as do good [20]. Populations rendered more vulnerable by poverty, abuse, disability, illness, infirmity or low social capital need especially strong protection from ineffective practice:

Frequently, people who use social work services are poorly educated or are on low incomes, and some are old and sick, but this is no reason why they should be subjected to practice interventions which have not been shown to be effective . . . Indeed, it can be argued that only practice that has been

---

[10] The notion that early intervention can result in measurable social and economic gains was strongly supported a century later. A key study of an influential American early intervention programme noted that: 'over the lifetime of the participants, the pre-school program returns to the public an estimated $7.16 for every dollar spent'. See Schweinhart, L; Barnes, H. and Weikart, D. (1993) *Significant Benefits: the High/Scope Perry pre-school study through age 27.* Ypsilanti, MI: High/Scope Press, p. xviii.

subject to rigorous effectiveness research can truly claim to be ethical practice [21].

A sound knowledge of the research base and the judicious use of practice methods based on current best evidence is, we would argue, a moral and ethical obligation of all those who aspire to professional status.

Most people manage their own financial affairs by purchasing items or services that give the greatest satisfaction for the least cost. Similarly, efficient use of public money is another reason to ensure that care is provided based on evidence of what is thought to work best for service users. Efficiency is an essential corollary of effectiveness. For example, an evaluation of a popular parent support programme found the service highly valued by mothers; however, less than half of those referred had made use of it, resulting in a substantial increase in the unit cost of its delivery [22]. Another way of thinking about effectiveness is the notion of 'number needed to treat' (NNT). If, for example, a programme designed to help adults with long term mental health problems find and retain employment for a minimum of 12 months has a consistent success rate of 20 per cent, it will have an NNT of five; that is, five people will have to enter the programme in order for one to experience success. Whether or not this will be considered satisfactory depends on the comparative effectiveness of other approaches, the severity of the problem, and the cost of doing nothing.[11] Evidence-based approaches can help identify which services are more effective at achieving particular outcomes, allowing value for money judgements to be made, and ensuring that resources are directed towards approaches offering the most promising long term, as well as more immediate outcomes.

How can we develop evidence-based practice?

In order to practice ethically and effectively, social workers must be able to integrate three crucial sources of information: the views and preferences of service users, their own professional judgement and the research base of the profession [23]. To achieve this synthesis, a number of core skills are necessary:

• *Formulating a practice question.* Asking a question is easy. Asking a question that can be answered meaningfully is harder. Asking a question that can be answered meaningfully and then applying the answer to practice is harder still. However, unless this skill can be learnt, evidence-based practice cannot become a reality.

---

[11] More information about NNT, including the calculations for many common ailments, can be viewed on the Bandolier website: *www.jr2.ox.ac.uk/bandolier/booth/booths/NNTs.html*.

- *Finding research evidence that can answer our question.* There are many sources of information in the evidential universe. Practitioners need to know where to find it, if necessary with help, as quickly and efficiently as possible.
- *Appraising research evidence.* Cars, domestic appliances and football teams are not equal in value or utility. Neither is research evidence. Some studies can be relied on more than others. Some kinds of evidence are more use than others. Practitioners should be able to distinguish between more and less valid and reliable research evidence, to identify which kinds of evidence are more and less useful for answering the question being asked, and to understand the criteria that must be applied in assessing research.
- *Applying the results to practice.* The relatively low profile of research in social work is partly a factor of a traditional bias in research production in the social sciences towards theoretical rather than applied studies. For the busy social worker this may mean being confronted with very long journal articles, with poor or non-existent abstracts which appear to have little bearing on downstream practice issues. However, much important research does exist that has direct implications for practice. Having found it and appraised it for quality, the next step is to consider how it can be used to affect practice positively.

This book, therefore, leans towards information that has direct relevance to the day to day tasks of social work and social care practitioners. This should not be taken to mean that we dismiss the importance of theory in favour of an exclusive focus on the effectiveness of interventions. Knowledge utilisation in social care, for example, depends on a number of factors of which the empirical research base of an intervention is unlikely to be always the most powerful [24]. Social workers are rightly concerned about the conceptual underpinnings of their profession. However, social work literature is not lacking in theory; rather it lacks critical attention to the development and evaluation of effective interventions, which comprises a small proportion of its published output [25].

Some cautionary tales

The cultivation of uncertainty is a basic principle of scientific inquiry. This has a number of implications for both practice and research production, as was noted almost two decades ago, not least that we:

> . . . affiliate less easily to schools and to new fashions; are less 'committed' but more discerning; that we have limited liability relationships with our theories rather than love affairs [26].

Knowledge acquisition is rarely a straightforward process; we may be required to modify our views or even our more deeply held beliefs when new information emerges, as these examples illustrate.

Life is never simple

All professions should accumulate a broader and better evidence base over time. However, this may often mean two steps forwards and one back, or several sideways. Evidence-based practice does not ignore, as is often believed, the complexity of human problems and their solutions. Stress, for example, is something that most practitioners (and probably more service users) are familiar with. For many decades, peptic ulcers were associated with stress, indeed an inflamed ulcer was the quintessential example of a stress related disease. Psychotherapists located the roots of stress in early childhood relationships, proposing that the mothers of ulcer sufferers were dominant and obsessional, and their fathers were unassertive and passive. Then, in 1983, a bacillus was found lurking in the stomach lining of sufferers – helicobacter pylori. The ulcer responded to antibiotics, and much schadenfreude was enjoyed by gastroenterologists at the discomfiture of stress theorists and psychotherapists, and not a little relief that messy psychosomatic explanations could be shown the door. Life, however, is rarely that simple. It was subsequently noted that many people with h. pylori did not develop ulcers, meaning that the bacillus could not be the sole causal factor. Stress had to be re-examined. It is now generally recognised that while stress alone is unlikely to cause a peptic ulcer, it may act as a contributory factor by increasing the production of gastric acid [27]. An evidence-based response to peptic ulcers will thus consider both physiological and emotional issues, and pharmacological and psychological responses, as well as acknowledging that there is very rarely a single explanation, or a single solution for the problems that confront the mish-mash of genes, experience, and environment from which all human beings are forged.

People don't always tell the truth

We often hear the expression 'people are experts on their own lives'. This may be so, but can the uncorroborated accounts of people involved in research studies always be relied upon? An excellent way of learning about people's lives is to ask them to keep diaries. However, memories are fallible and diaries are more reliable (though sometimes less enjoyable) when they describe events that have just happened, rather than when the account is written some days or weeks later. The intensity and frequency of chronic pain for example, can be mapped by sufferers keeping a diary of their condition at designated times each day. When two groups of patients were asked to do this, one using personal organisers, the other electronic palm computers, the results showed similar levels of compliance. The two groups recorded pretty much the same number of diary entries, at the times the entry was supposed to be made. The palm computers electronically recorded the time of diary entry and hence were a 'true' record. The personal organiser relied on the truthfulness of the patient. However, unknown to the group using the personal organisers, a photosensor with the capacity to detect light was inserted in the organiser, thus enabling the research team to know when the diary had *really* been opened, rather than when the patient said it had been opened. The results? Reported compliance of the personal organiser group was over 90 per cent, yet the photosensitive strip recorded no openings at all on a third of the days [28]. Many of the accounts were retrospective, not contemporaneous. Some patients had been fibbing.[12]

Users sometimes get it wrong

Shortly before World War Two, Dr Richard Clarke Cabot conceived of a study which would test the widely held belief that identifying young people thought to be at risk of offending, and offering preventive programmes, would help keep youngsters out of trouble. Almost 300 boys, aged under 10 years, were identified from the towns of Cambridge and Somerville in Massachusetts, USA. Care was taken to avoid the programme just being identified as one for 'bad' children. The 300 boys were assessed, matched to another of similar age, social background and temperament. By the toss of a coin, they were allocated to a treatment group, which received individual help from case workers, family support and referral where necessary to specialists, and a control group, who received no additional help. Visits were made to the boys in the treatment group, on average, twice a month for almost six years. The composition of the groups was re-examined after several years to ensure no significant differences had emerged. None had. When the programme ended in 1945, boys in the treatment

---

[12] There is a further lesson to be learnt from this example, and that is the need to take possible sources of bias into account when appraising evidence. Three of the study authors were directors of a company which provides electronic diary support for clinical trials.

group had received extra tuition, medical and psychiatric treatment, been to summer camps, participated in sporting events and had been enlisted in community programmes. At the conclusion of the programme, many of the boys thought to be at risk of maladjustment were reported as doing much better than expected. So far, so good. In the late 1970s, the boys in the treatment group – now middle aged men – were tracked down and questioned about the programme benefits. Two-thirds reported a range of ways in which they believed it had benefited them, including diverting them from crime and creating lasting friendships. So far, even better. But this was not the end of the story. Court, mental hospital, alcohol treatment facility and death records were searched. The results? Compared to members of the control group, members of the treatment group were more likely to have been convicted of a crime, to have died, on average, five years earlier and were more likely to have been diagnosed as alcoholic, schizophrenic, or manic-depressive. And there was more bad news. Boys who had been visited most frequently, whose families were the most co-operative, and were in the programme the longest, did worst [29].

Different strokes, different folks

So what lessons can be drawn from these tales? That life is just too complicated for a discipline like social work to develop an evidence base which may be applied consistently? That all evidence is unreliable? That different people's perspectives on what is convincing evidence are irreconcilable? We would beg to differ. Our conclusion would be that there is never a 'final' answer to a problem, just one that is the best for the time being; that plausible new explanations should be considered when they emerge; that social care practice must be willingly exposed to critical inspection; that intimate personal exposure to an issue can bring both illumination and delusion; that much loved theories should be discarded or amended if flaws emerge and that most importantly of all, we should remain curious.

The right tool for the right job

Social work is a profession committed to equality. Much of its mission involves challenging inequalities, identifying the causes of unequal outcomes, and developing strategies to minimise difference, especially when the root cause is discrimination or social injustice. This often makes practitioners uncomfortable with approaches which value some kinds of information or knowledge

Table 1.2 Different kinds of research questions

Questions about context	Questions about outcomes
Why do some people repeatedly harm themselves?	What is the most effective way to prevent repeated episodes of self-harm?
Why are many men reluctant to attend programmes at family centres?	How can male attrition rates in family centre programmes be reduced?
Why do some disabled people prefer not to take advantage of direct payment schemes?	What is the effect of direct payment schemes on the incomes of disabled people?
How do elderly people feel about being relocated from one residential setting to another?	What is the effect on mortality rates of relocating elderly people from one residential setting to another?
What are the views of boarded-out children on educational incentive payments to foster carers?	Will paying supplements to foster carers contingent upon examination success improve the academic performance of boarded-out children?
What is the range of opinions held by adults with learning disabilities about the respective merits of residential village accommodation and 'ordinary' housing?	Are health and well-being scores of adults with learning disabilities in residential village accommodation superior to similar adults living in 'ordinary' housing?

over others. A great deal of discussion has taken place on the relative merits of different types of knowledge, a highly positive result of which has been the transfer of service users' views from the margin to centre stage [30]. While many legitimate objections have been made to the hegemony of certain types of knowledge, and of certain types of experts, an evidence-based approach implies an inescapable assertion. *Not all kinds of evidence are equal in value.* A rapid qualification, however, is required. The value of any piece of information depends entirely on the *kind* of question we are trying to answer. In many situations, where the main aim is to understand the context of a situation, the evidential weight of personal testimony will be far greater than any number of quantitative studies, or the opinions of 'experts'. Without the testimony of service users, we may still be able to answer the question 'what works?', but not the more important question, 'what matters?' [31]. We cannot begin to explore people's circumstances without listening carefully to their narratives. But what if the questions asked are concerned with the effects on people of an intervention? In such cases, more value might be attached to different kinds of evidence. As illustrated in Table 1.2, the value of any item of 'evidence' all depends on the kind of information required to answer a given practice question.

All these questions are important and worthy of investigation, but need to be answered by different approaches. Both kinds of questions require a distinction to be made between weaker and stronger evidence in a transparent way. However, questions on *outcomes* have occupied far less attention from both social work practitioners and researchers, and it is in the field of outcome or impact studies that the need to consider *levels* of evidential weight becomes most acute.

Not all evidence is born equal

If we want to investigate the extent to which a certain intervention or event is associated with a particular outcome, the question can be approached in a number of ways. All approaches have their strengths and weaknesses, some may be impossible to use in some circumstances and others will be unable to answer the question we have posed.

A fuller discussion of the respective merits of different approaches to answering a research question can be found in Chapter 3. However as illustrated in Table 1.3 some sorts of information can provide a higher level of certainty than others that an intervention is likely to lead to a particular outcome. Similarly, certain kinds of investigation are more useful than others for answering some questions. It can also be seen that not all methods are practical, possible or ethical when investigating certain kinds of issues. When information from a variety of sources reaches a similar conclusion, the level of confidence in the findings increases. Confidence is also related to the volume and strength of evidence. For example, practitioners would not be expected to abandon a widely accepted method of working on the basis of contradictory evidence from a single, small randomised controlled trial. Equally, a rapid reassessment of an approach would be anticipated if there was widespread and consistent opposition from service users. However, where the nature of the problem permits, the strongest evidence on social work *interventions* will come from randomised controlled trials, and from systematic reviews or meta-analyses,[13] which are able to aggregate data from large numbers of trials and other robust studies.

---

[13] A very clear description of meta-analysis can be accessed at: *http://www.informedhealthon-line.org/item.aspx?tabid=26&pagerequest=2*

The power of experiments

If you wanted to compare the nutritional value of different dietary regimes, you could just ask people what they ate, how it made them feel, and record the answers. However, you would have no independent means of checking the accuracy of your respondents' replies, or even whether they were telling the truth. (Food intake rivals sexual activity as a source of self-delusion.) Alternatively, you might define your outcome measures, recruit several groups who would eat the different diets, ensure that strict compliance with the regimes was observed and agree what period of time you wished the trial to run. Well, it's been done before.

Please test your servants for ten days. Give us nothing but vegetables to eat and water to drink. Then compare our appearance with that of the young men who eat the royal food, and treat your servants in accordance with what you see. So he agreed to this and tested them for ten days. At the end of the ten days they looked healthier and better nourished than any of the young men who ate the royal food. So the guard took away their choice food and the wine they were to drink and gave them vegetables instead.

(Daniel 1:12–16)

You might be more convinced if the two groups had been randomly selected, and some rather more robust post-intervention measures taken. But the evidence was good enough for Nebuchadnezzar, thus providing one of the earliest examples of research utilisation.

More recently, but still some two and a half centuries ago, a rather more vigorous study of food intake and its impact on health was carried out; it changed the course of history. Long maritime voyages prior to the mid-eighteenth century were plagued by the highly debilitating illness of scurvy, caused by a deficiency of vitamin C, which is found in fresh fruit and vegetables. In May 1747, on board the *Salisbury*, James Lind took 12 patients with scurvy, their cases being 'as similar as I could have them', ordered them in six pairs, and provided six different treatments, each of which had its advocates of effectiveness. These included cider; elixir vitriol; vinegar; sea water; a mixture of nutmeg, garlic and mustard seed; and two oranges and one lemon, all to be given daily for six days:

The consequence was, the most sudden and visible good effects were perceived from the use of the oranges and lemons; one of those who had taken them being at the end of six days fit for duty . . . the other was the best recovered of any in his condition; and now being deemed pretty well, was appointed nurse to the rest of the sick [32].

This study contained most key elements of the experimental approach; an important question, equivalent groups, no obvious known advantage of one treatment over another, and careful exposure to the treatments according to

Table 1.3　Strengths and weaknesses of different kinds of evidence

Source of evidence	Description	Strengths	Weaknesses
Personal testimony	Account by a person intimately acquainted with or affected by a particular issue.	Powerful and immediate; may give vivid insights into events concealed from much of the population.	Difficult to verify; may lead to inflation of prevalence; accounts of distressing personal trauma may inhibit critical appraisal.
Practice experience	Accumulated wisdom from repeated exposure to similar situations or problems.	Enables practitioners to identify anomalous situations where counter-intuitive decisions can and should be made.	Errors can be consistently repeated unless tested by other sources of evidence; hard for lay people to challenge.
Single case design	Repeated standardised measurement of a client's situation or problems over time.	Easy and practical; can be used by practitioners with minimal training; clients are able to collaborate and contribute.	More difficult to apply with non-behavioural interventions; absence of controls weakens attribution of cause and effect.
Client opinion study	Narrative or survey accounts of user views or reported needs.	Valuable insights from those at the receiving end; compels professionals to stay focused on the client's priorities.	Correlation between satisfaction and achievement of service aims is low; needs described by clients may not translate into actual service use.
Cross-sectional study	A representative sample of people are surveyed at one point in time.	Survey can be repeated at intervals, illustrating changing trends over time.	May be hard to detect why changes have occurred; difficult to observe trends in minority populations.

Method	Description	Strengths	Weaknesses
Cohort study	The same sample of people are surveyed over several points in time, sometimes from childhood to maturity.	Best source of evidence on association between childhood experience and adult outcomes; can give powerful support for certain early interventions.	Data often emerge too late for effective policy making; study members may drop out over time; very expensive approach when maintained over decades.
Quasi-experimental study	Different interventions are offered; no random allocation to groups; use of natural populations or case matching.	Powerful method of exploring the impact of an intervention when randomisation is impossible; can be applied to communities as well as groups.	Difficulty in ensuring equivalence of groups and natural changes in group composition over time can result in less reliable findings.
Randomised controlled trial (RCT)	One group receives an intervention, another receives none or an intervention of another type; the chance of being allocated to either group is identical.	Changes in the client's situation can be attributed to the intervention with a high degree of confidence; best approach for controlling bias.	Mistakes in randomisation can invalidate results; cannot be applied to many important social problems; without equipoise – an equal chance that benefits will occur in both groups – ethical difficulties may arise.
Systematic review Meta-analysis	Aggregation of results from eligible studies; eligibility criteria defined in advance (usually but not necessarily RCTs); review methodology is replicable.	Best source of reassurance that an intervention works (or doesn't); meta-analysis pools numerical results; large reviews carry great statistical power; can be applied to any kind of data.	Requires a substantial number of robust primary studies in a given area; methodology less well developed for synthesising qualitative data; results may be hard to apply in specific cases.

a protocol decided in advance. While many important questions cannot be explored through this approach, its potential remains greatly underused within the field of social care [33].

Validity

All methods of investigation are a trade-off between internal and external validity. *Internal validity* measures whether a hypothesis stands up under the conditions in which it is tested – does it work in the lab? *External validity* measures the extent to which it can be generalised to other similar situations – does it work in the real world? For example, you may set out to evaluate an intervention in a pilot project, where resources are ring-fenced, staff morale is high, skilled specialists are easily recruited and retained, intensive training is provided, political support is forthcoming and clients are attracted by the innovative approach. The results may be positive. But will it work as well when extended more widely, where staff absences and recruitment, resources, client motivation and political commitment are closer to what is more typically found? If not, your findings will have low external validity, and more importantly, the intervention may have little practical application.

Stories and numbers

There will always be irreconcilable conflicts between different sources of 'evidence'. Perhaps the most important source of dissonance is the collision between the perspectives of people who deal with numbers and those who deal with narrative, that is, quantitative and qualitative approaches. This is particularly pertinent in social work, as social care practitioners are usually more comfortable with, and more affected by, stories than statistics. Narrative approaches deal with flesh and blood, real people who have moving stories to tell. Quantitative studies largely deal with impersonal numbers. An emotional account of how a particular procedure saved someone's life may carry more persuasive weight than a statistical table suggesting that, overall, the procedure causes more harm than good. There are a number of reasons for this [34]. First, the power of stories enables the storyteller and the listener to form a bond, and bonds are jeopardised by scepticism. Second, vivid narratives, especially of traumatic or distressing events, tend to result in listeners overestimating the probability of such events occurring. A preventive intervention is thus often demanded, regardless of whether any effective option actually exists. Last, human brains appear better equipped to process narratives than numerical inputs. For example, advocacy groups tend to be far more uncritically supportive of universal screening procedures for cancers than medical practitioners [35]. The former constituency will tend to be more influenced by stories of people whose tumours were detected by early screening, and who believe, often passionately, that preventive screening should be made available to all. The latter constituency will be more concerned with the consequences of false positive diagnoses, and unnecessarily aggressive treatment of low grade tumours. In this, and in other situations, the power of personal narrative collides with a numerical expression of which procedure is likely to result in the greater overall health gain. There is no easy resolution to these dilemmas, but an understanding of the processes that may lead practitioners, and service users, to favour one source of knowledge over another is necessary for sensitive evidence-based decision making.

Levels of evidence

We have argued that some forms of evidence may be stronger and more reliable than others. This can be illustrated with an example of an extremely common problem. One of the biggest causes of morbidity in developed countries is depressive illness. Up to a third of people will experience depression, and most of the population, if not affected directly, will be touched by the illness of someone close to them. Depression is an illness that responds to a wide range of treatments, depending on its intensity and the circumstances of the person affected. Is it possible to say which treatment is the most effective? A common classification system is to consider the evidence for a particular intervention or treatment as strong, moderate or weak, using a pre-defined method of assessment, as illustrated in Table 1.4.

Not all practitioners nor mental health service users will agree with these judgements and indeed, despite this continuum of 'strong', 'moderate' and 'weak', all the treatments in this table have been found to enjoy at least *some* measure of support in trials when compared to non-intervention. However, our greater confidence in some of these treatments as opposed to others is that some have been tested in a greater number of high quality studies, containing a larger number of people, producing more consistently positive results, more of the time. This does not mean of course that any particular individual may not experience greater benefit from a treatment carrying less evidential weight, nor indeed that the evidence base for some treatments will not weaken with the passage of time, while others may be strengthened. Indeed, the evidence base of non-directive counselling in cases of mild to moderate depression has strengthened in the past few years, being classified as of 'unknown effectiveness' in earlier versions of *Clinical Evidence* [36]. It is also the case that some kinds of interventions draw far more research attention and funding than others. Complementary therapies, for example, rarely attract the kind of research investment that is routinely directly towards the testing of new pharmaceutical products. This is a legitimate criticism.

Table 1.4 Treatments for depression: relative effectiveness based on evidence from clinical trials

Beneficial	Likely to be beneficial	Unknown effectiveness
Tricyclic and heterocyclic antidepressants (in mild to moderate and severe depression)	St John's Wort (in mild to moderate depression)	Cognitive therapy (severe depression)
Monoamine oxidase inhibitors (as above)	Problem solving treatment (in mild to moderate depression)	Interpersonal psychotherapy (severe depression)
Selective serotonin reuptake inhibitors (as above)	Combined drug and psychological treatment (in mild to moderate and severe depression)	Problem solving treatment (severe depression)
Cognitive therapy (in mild to moderate depression)	Non-directive counselling (in mild to moderate depression)	Exercise (mild to moderate depression)
Interpersonal psychotherapy (in mild to moderate depression)	Care pathways (in mild to moderate depression)	Befriending (mild to moderate depression)
Electroconvulsive therapy (in severe depression)		Bibliotherapy[14] (mild to moderate depression)

Source: *Clinical Evidence* [36]

Another common criticism, especially pertinent to social care, is that where interventions involve considerable interpersonal contact, characteristics of the professional such as personality or gender, rather than any theoretical orientation is often of greater importance to client outcome, and this factor is given insufficient weight. This is another legitimate point, and has some support from the evidence base [37,38]. You might also think that some consideration of external factors is missing in considering how we might respond to depression; for example, having a rewarding job, a supportive family, a community strong in social capital, and being free from discrimination, poverty, physical pain, abuse and stress are all factors which appear to

---

[14] Directed reading of optimistic or spiritually rich material.

protect against depression. To simply treat a woman suffering from a depressive disorder, while ignoring the regular beatings she receives from a violent partner would be neither ethical nor effective. However, neither would simply focusing on family relationships while refusing to address the immediate problem. For example, as was noted a century ago, suicide rates are associated with broader social context and not just individual pathology. It is important to be aware of this, and this knowledge is significant when we are considering public health strategies. However, a practitioner is unlikely to help an individual client with suicidal ideation very much by just reading Durkheim. Understanding the structural factors underpinning human suffering is of great importance, but skills and techniques that can deal with the immediacy of people's problems are also needed.

What difference does it all make?

The impact of the 'evidence-based' approach on the delivery of social care services, let alone the welfare of service users, is as yet unknown. Nonetheless, the potential impact of a 'what works?' agenda on human services is substantial, as may be seen from the example of the UK probation service. Up to the mid-1980s, the weight of research evidence appeared to indicate that rehabilitative strategies had little effect on offending behaviour [39]. However, several meta-analyses of criminal justice began to provide policy makers with convincing evidence that intensive supervision, with the focus on the offence rather than the offender, could achieve significant reductions in recidivism [40]. As a result, an evidence-based platform of intervention was devised and more emphasis was placed on programme integrity (meaning that the programme was carried out as intended). The changes may not have been to everyone's liking, but there is a broad consensus that the result has been an increased perception of professionalism, and enhanced status in relation to other parts of the criminal justice system [41]. And if the acquisition of status appears to be a self-indulgent aspiration for the social care practitioner, we might wish to consider what kind of practitioner other than one of high status we would choose for ourselves.

Another example is the genesis and development of the national Sure Start programme. Probably the largest early years investment of its type in British history, the evidence base of Sure Start rests on a small number of influential randomised controlled trials which showed highly promising results. Children who participated in programmes attained significantly better outcomes, in terms of scholastic achievement, health, work, social stability and crime avoidance, than similar children who did not. It is unlikely that policy makers would have been persuaded to make a multi-million pound investment if the

LIB

evidence base had rested on professional opinion, studies lacking control groups, or service user testimony alone [42].

One of the biggest contributions that evidence-based practice can make to a profession is that it generates a common language and set of operating principles. Once agreement can be reached (mostly, if not entirely) on the principles that govern what is stronger and weaker evidence, then energy can be invested in testing and improving interventions rather than arguing about epistemology.

The law of large numbers

Most interventions in health and social care are primarily concerned with loading the odds as strongly as possible in favour of the service user. However, because benefits for any one individual may not always be large and visible – though these are the cases that are most likely to be remembered and described – the effects of interventions on large populations may need to be examined in order to detect differences in service user outcomes. For example, making additional resources available in a specific care setting to help looked after children complete homework may only result in a slight increase in an overall GCSE pass rate. You might conclude that this was just coincidence, or natural variation, and feel that the investment of extra effort was not worth it. However, if this effect were aggregated across all 60,000 children currently looked after in England, a substantial overall improvement in children's educational attainments might be detected. Evidence-based practice is not a silver bullet. It is simply, as we have argued, about trying to increase the probability that successful outcomes will occur.

Individual client preferences, the resources available and the skills and knowledge of the practitioner will always remain crucial factors. However, the 'value added' by evidence-based practice rests on the claim that when applied consistently, evidence-based approaches are more likely to yield positive outcomes than approaches which have no such basis in evidence [43]. This proposition of course, needs to be evaluated over time, and the best test is a tangible and measurable increase in positive outcomes for service users.

Challenging claims to authority

People who use social care services are often the poorest, least well educated and most disadvantaged of our citizens. Throughout history, and despite the best of intentions, some activities by social welfare services have made people sicker, unhappier and poorer – or at least, have done less good than they might have done. An evidence-based approach involves fair but robust scrutiny of claims to authority. Sources claiming authority who object to their views being scrutinised or challenged, whether they are from lay or professional communities, can be described as *authoritarian*.

'Claims to authority' depend on expertise of one kind or another, but they include:

Expert knowledge

I have conducted a systematic review of all trials that evaluate treatment programmes for sexual offenders with learning disabilities. My outcome measures are programme drop-out rate and recidivism. I conclude that a combination of cognitive behavioural therapy and anti-libidinal medication is the most effective intervention.

How might these claims be tested? We might ask – was your search strategy adequate? How did you define 'learning disability'? How much variation was there in the results? Was the statistical analysis sound? How many offenders would have to be treated in order to achieve one success? Is this approach effective in all settings, and across all cultural groups? Were the views of the participants sought? Can the results actually be applied to practice?

Practice experience

I have worked with bereaved children for 20 years. The loss of a parent or close relative, especially a sibling, can result in depression, a decline in school performance, sleeplessness and, in younger children, panic attacks, bed-wetting and tantrums. I strongly believe that all bereaved children should be offered counselling and contact in managed settings with other bereaved children. Failure to offer support may result in long term emotional damage.

Similarly, we might ask – are these views on the long term effects of bereavement supported from sources such as cohort studies? What proportion of bereaved children suffers from diagnosable psychological disorders? Is this significantly higher than in the general population? Are there any circumstances where harm could result from the offer of help? If some children are more at risk than others, is there any way of identifying which and with what degree of accuracy? How many children would recover without help?

Personal experience

My daughter was approached in an internet chat room by someone pretending to be her age, but who turned out to be an older man who propositioned her for sex. She says that this happens all the time to her friends. There needs to be urgent action to stop this menace. All schools should introduce awareness programmes, stricter controls should be built into computer software, and parents should not allow children to use chatrooms unsupervised, or have computers in their bedrooms. Unmoderated chatrooms should be closed.

Claims based on personal experience must be tested also. We might ask – how prevalent is this? Are there any independent sources of data? What are the opportunity costs of a large scale intervention programme? What are the relevant merits of learning to deal with the problem or being protected from it? What are the views of children on this matter? Will there be any unintended consequences?

Belief systems

Cochlear implants are promoted against the wishes of people in the Deaf community. We have our own culture and our own means of communication. Invasive attempts to artificially create 'hearing' deny the validity of our way of life and who we are, and imply that we are incomplete or flawed. They should not be encouraged.

Those outside specific communities, especially those with a history of discrimination or oppression, can sometimes be inhibited from challenging strongly held beliefs like this. However, this view also constitutes a claim to authority, and must be subjected to a similar critical process. We might ask – what range of views on this issue are there among people who are hearing impaired? What are the views of those who have had, and refused implants? Is there any evidence that implants result in significant health or social benefits (or deficits)? Do the views of those with congenital hearing impairment on this issue differ from those who have lost hearing through illness or trauma?

In all these cases, challenging views which claim to be authoritative is necessary for the continuous building of a sound evidence base. Activities most likely to do good rather than harm tend to be supported by a range of sources, expert, professional, personal and political, not just by a single source. All forms of authority should be open to critical appraisal – constituencies promoting user-led, alternative approaches have as much potential for authoritarianism as mainstream professionals [44].

Conclusion

Out of the crooked timber of humanity no straight thing was ever made [45].

The reader should now be clear about what evidence-based practice is and what it isn't, and what this approach can and can't do. What it can't do is provide a set of conclusive and universally applicable answers to practice problems. What it doesn't do, and is emphatically not trying to do, is to diminish professional experience or subvert the centrality of service user perspectives. What evidence-based practice can do is help us compare the respective claims of competing approaches, and by combining this knowledge with the views of the people we serve and our professional experience, make the best possible decisions about the welfare of service users. Evidence-based practice, in both challenging authoritarian views, and demanding that sources of authority justify their positions, is part of a long and honourable radical tradition in social work. We hope that the reader has been persuaded that while a commitment to evidence-based practice brings new challenges, some dangers, and not inconsiderable demands, it also offers the possibility of legitimising social work and social care in a new and exciting way.

References

[1] Preston-Shoot, M. (2002) Why social workers don't read. *Care and Health Guide*. 11, March 10–12.
[2] Swinkels, A., Albarran, J.W., Means, R.I., Mitchell, T. and Stewart, M.C. (2002) Evidence-based practice in health and social care: where are we now? *Journal of Interprofessional Care*. 16: 4, 335–47.
[3] Department of Health (1998) *Modernising Social Services*. Cm 4169, London: The Stationery Office.
[4] General Social Care Council (2002) *Codes of Practice*. London: General Social Care Council.
[5] Horwath, J. with Thurlow, C. (2004) Preparing students for evidence-based child and family social work: an experimental learning approach. *Social Work Education*. 23: 1, 7–24.
[6] British Association of Social Workers (2002) *The Code of Ethics for Social Work*. Brighton: BASW.
[7] National Association of Social Workers (1996) *Code of Ethics*. Washington DC: NASW.
[8] Myers, L.L. and Thyer, B.A. (1997) Should social work clients have the right to effective treatment? *Social Work*. 42: 3, 288–98.
[9] Rosen, A., Proctor, E.K. and Staudt, M.M. (1999) Social work research and the quest for effective practice. *Social Work Research*. 23: 4–14.
[10] Sheldon, B. and Macdonald, G. (1999) *Research and Practice in Social Care: Mind the Gap*. Exeter: Centre for Evidence-based Social Services.
[11] Department of Health (1998) *Modernising Social Services*. Cm 4169, London: The Stationery Office.
[12] Sackett, D.L., Rosenberg, W.M., Gray, J.A., Haynes, R.B. and Richardson, W.S. (1996) Evidence based medicine: what it is and what it isn't. *British Medical Journal*. 312: 71–2, 71.
[13] Greenhalgh, T. (1999) Narrative based medicine in an evidence based world. *British Medical Journal*. 318: 323–5.
[14] Chalmers, I. (1995) What do I want from health research and researchers when I am a patient? *British Medical Journal*. 310: 1315–8.

[15] Crisp, B.R., Anderson, M.R., Orme, J. and Lister, P.G. (2003) *Learning and Teaching in Social Work Education: Assessment*, Knowledge Review No. 1. London: Social Care Institute for Excellence.

[16] Antfilogof, S. (2002) *Focus on the Future: Key Messages From Focus Groups About the Future of Social Work Training.* London: DoH.

[17] Richmond, M. (1917) *Social Diagnosis.* New York: Russell Sage Foundation.

[18] Night and Day (September 1897). Cited in Rose, J. (1987) *For the Sake of the Children.* London: Hodder and Stoughton.

[19] Cochrane, A. (1972) *Effectiveness and Efficiency: Random Reflections of Health Services.* Nuffield Hospitals Provincial Trust. Reprinted 1989 in association with British Medical Journal.

[20] Gambrill, E. (1997) *Social Work Practice: A Critical Thinker's Guide.* Oxford: Oxford University Press.

[21] Ainsworth, F. and Hansen, P. (2002) Evidence-based social work: a reachable goal? *Social Work and Social Sciences Review.* 10: 2, 35–48.

[22] Oakley, A., Mauthner, M., Rajan, L. and Turner, H. (1996) Supporting vulnerable families: an evaluation of NEWPIN. *Health Visitor.* 68: 188–91.

[23] Howard, M.O., McMillen, C.J. and Pollio, D.E. (2003) Teaching evidence-based practice: towards a new paradigm for social work education. *Research on Social Work Practice.* 13: 2, 234–59.

[24] Marsh, J.C. (2003) Chewing on cardboard and other pleasures of knowledge utilisation. *Social Work.* 48: 3, 293–4.

[25] Fortune, A.E. and Proctor, E.K. (2001) Research on social work interventions (editorial). *Social Work Research.* 25: 2, 67–9.

[26] Sheldon, B. (1986) Social work effectiveness experiments: review and implications. *British Journal of Social Work.* 16: 223–42.

[27] Levenstein, S. (1998) Stress and peptic ulcer: life beyond helicobacter. *British Medical Journal.* 316: 538–41.

[28] Stone, A.A., Shiffman, S., Schwartz, J.E., Broderick, J.E. and Hufford, M.R. (2002) Patient non-compliance with paper diaries. *British Medical Journal.* 324: 1193–4.

[29] McCord, J. (1992) The Cambridge-Somerville study: a pioneering longitudinal-experimental study of delinquency prevention. In McCord, J. and Tremblay, R.E. (Eds.) *Preventing Antisocial Behaviour: Interventions From Birth Through Adolescence.* New York: Gilford Press.

[30] Pawson, R., Boaz, A., Grayson, L., Long, A. and Barnes, C. (2003) *Types and Quality of Knowledge in Social Care.* Knowledge Review No. 3. London: SCIE (available at: *www.scie.org.uk*).

[31] Glass, N. (2001) What works for children: the political issues. *Children and Society.* 15: 14–20.

[32] *www.jameslindlibrary.org/trial_records/17th_18th_Century/lind/lind_kp.html* Accessed 20.04.04.

[33] Newman, T. and Roberts, H. (1997) Assessing social work effectiveness in child care practice: the contribution of randomized controlled trials. *Child: Health, Care and Development.* 23, 4: 287–96.

[34] Newman, T.B. (2003) The power of stories over statistics. *British Medical Journal.* 327: 1424–7.

[35] Jørgenson, K.J. and Gøtzsche, P.C. (2004) Presentation on websites of possible benefits and harms from screening for breast cancer: cross sectional study. *British Medical Journal.* 328: 148–51.

[36] Clinical Evidence. *www.clinicalevidence.com*. Treatments for depressive disorders. July 2002. Accessed 15.04.04.

[37] Roter, D.L., Hall, J.A. and Aoki, Y. (2002) Physician gender effects in medical communication: a meta-analytical review. *Journal of the American Medical Association*. 288: 756–64.

[38] Okiishi, J., Lambert, M.J., Nielson, S.L. and Ogles, B.M. (2003) Waiting for the supershrink: an empirical analysis of therapist effects. *Clinical Psychology and Psychotherapy*. 10: 6, 361–73.

[39] Blagg, H. and Smith, D. (1989) *Crime, Penal Policy and Social Work*. London: Longman.

[40] Lipsey, M.W. (1999) What do we learn from 400 research studies on the effectiveness of treatment with juvenile delinquents? In McGuire, J. (Ed.) *What Works? Reducing Offending: Guidelines From Research and Practice*. Chichester: John Wiley.

[41] Newman, J. and Nutley, S. (2003) Transforming the probation service: 'what works', organisational change and professional identity. *Policy and Politics*. 31: 4, 547–63.

[42] NESS Research Team (2004) The national evaluation of sure start local programmes in England. *Child and Adolescent Mental Health*. 9: 1, 2–8.

[43] Reid, W.J. (1997) Evaluating the dodo's verdict: do all interventions have equivalent outcomes? *Social Work Research*. 21: 1, 5–16.

[44] Chalmers, I. (1983) Scientific inquiry and authoritarianism in perinatal care and education. *Birth*. 10: 3, 151–64.

[45] Kant, I. cited in Berlin, I. (1998) *The Proper Study of Mankind: An Anthology of Essays*. Pimlico: London.

Chapter 2

Locating the Evidence: Finding What Matters, and Not Finding What Doesn't

This chapter discusses:
- Formulating a search question relevant to practice.
- Identifying the most suitable sources of evidence.[1]
- How to search databases.
- Refining a search.

'Would you tell me please, which way I ought to go from here?'
'That depends a good deal on where you want to get to', said the Cat.
(Alice's Adventures in Wonderland)

In this chapter we take you through the process of locating research relevant to social care practice. By the end of the chapter, we hope you will be in a position to conduct your own searches effectively. We discuss how to formulate a research question which may answer a practice problem. We then introduce the main sources of social care research, highlighting the strengths and limitations of each. We cover libraries, grey literature, key websites, gateways, search engines, statistical sources, journals and databases. Lastly, we describe how to create and refine a search strategy to enable you to find the information you need. Some worked examples of database searches are provided towards the end of the chapter. In conjunction with this chapter, you may wish to refer to the last section of the book, which acts as a resource guide, providing an extensive list of journals, websites and databases.

---

[1] All URLs (Universal Resource Locators), or website addresses, cited in this chapter were checked on 27/07/04.

Net benefits

Schools of social work in both the UK [1] and the USA [2] have devoted comparatively little attention to teaching students how to search for and locate practice or research information from online (internet based) databases. Combined with a residual fear that excessive reliance on information technology will dehumanise the profession [3] and the severe practical problems reported by social workers in gaining access to research information [4,5], there are significant barriers of attitudes, competencies and resources. However, familiarity with both the research literature in a practitioner's field of expertise, and the methods needed to access it, are an indispensable part of a social worker's claim to professional status.

Achieving such familiarity is no longer possible without a working knowledge of databases and other internet resources. The internet is now a hugely important resource for locating evidence, as we seek to demonstrate in the course of this chapter. Complex database searches may require specialist training or the help of a librarian. However, simple searches of the most important databases relevant to social work, and knowledge of what these databases contain, is achievable by any practitioner with access to a PC and a modem. Similarly, familiarity with a few key websites containing social care research can open up access to a significant amount of freely available and relevant material without demanding considerable amounts of time or technical expertise.

Given the importance of the internet for locating social care research, those who are new to the internet may want to consult one of the many online, introductory guides. One of the most useful ones for social workers can be found on the Social Sciences Information Gateway (SOSIG).[2] For a basic starter guide on the technical aspects of the internet (including using PDF, internet browsers, how to use the toolbar etc.), social care staff can also use the web tutorials section of the Centre for Evidence-Based Social Services' 'be-evidence-based' resource.[3]

The second part of this chapter is essentially a resource guide which highlights the main sources of social care research online and elsewhere. However, as the cat from Alice in Wonderland puts it, the first thing to do before you work out which way to go, is to decide where you want to get to. As a social worker trying to locate research to guide your practice, the most important thing is to be clear about what exactly it is you want to find out. Aimless searching on the internet can make you feel overloaded with information. Similar frustration can arise when you just cannot seem to find

---

[2] *www.sosig.ac.uk/vts/social-research-methods/start.htm*
[3] *www.be-evidence-based.com/secure_pages/bebdev/training.html*

the information you need. Both these scenarios are less likely to occur if you are clear in your mission. The first section of this chapter is therefore devoted to formulating a 'research question'.

Asking questions

Librarians, information officers and researchers are frequently approached by practitioners, managers and policy makers – and sometimes people who use services – with questions they want answered in relation to some aspect of social welfare. The potential kinds of information they are looking for is obviously infinite, but tends to cluster into five main areas:

- Statistical or demographic information, for example, national or regional prevalence figures of specific client groups, data from large national surveys such as the decennial Census or official data from government sources.
- Information about innovative practice in a specific field of interest being carried out elsewhere in the UK, and sometimes in other countries, for example, the management of key worker schemes, carer support groups, family group conferences, multi-agency projects or self-advocacy schemes.
- Information about the aetiology of a condition, for example, Attention Deficit Hyperactivity Disorder (ADHD), dementia or Down's Syndrome.
- Information about the outcomes of strategies or approaches that are currently being delivered or are planned on the welfare of clients.
- Information about the views and experiences of those who use services.

What level of information do we require?

In formulating the question, we also need to consider the level of discretion exercised by the person wanting the information. For example, the effect of delayed discharge of older people from acute hospital wards on overall A&E waiting times will be of interest to senior civil servants when social and health care strategies are being considered. A research question exploring this issue will therefore be relevant to senior hospital or social care managers who are charged with meeting government targets. However, this question is of limited practical use to most social workers, who are more likely to need information on effective ways of helping rehabilitate older people leaving hospital. We thus need to consider whether we require information at the micro-, meso- or macro-level.

Practitioners tend to need micro-level information. They may ask, for example:

- How can we moderate the impact of parental separation on children?
- What are the most reliable tools for assessing mental health needs?
- How can we identify attachment problems between mothers and children in infancy?

Managers are more likely to need meso-level information, and may ask, for example:
- What model of short breaks for carers delivers the best outcomes for the lowest costs?
- What types of assistive devices are most helpful for enabling frail elderly people to bathe themselves?
- What are the most effective ways of enabling young parents to participate in child protection procedures?

Macro-level information will tend to be of most use to policy makers, who may ask, for example:
- Do parenting programmes reduce the prevalence of anti-social behaviour amongst young people?
- Do disabled children achieve better educational results in inclusive schools?
- Will the take up rate of direct payment schemes by disabled adults justify the costs of scheme implementation and maintenance?

Formulating questions about outcomes and processes

Questions may address process issues – *how* we go about doing things – or outcomes – the *impact* our activities have on service users. While process issues are extremely important, social work has traditionally paid comparatively little attention to *outcomes*. Questions about process need to consider what contribution – if any – effective processes make to outcomes. For example, the justification for promoting better inter-agency collaboration in child protection cases is that we believe it will result in fewer children being harmed or children suffering less harm. While the views of those involved in a programme designed to enhance inter-agency co-operation on the process are important, the best indicator of success is any change in the status of the service user.

Formulating a useful question about *outcomes* involves three stages. We need to ask:
- *Who* is the question about? (the population)
- *Which* strategy, intervention or activity are we considering? (the intervention), and is it being compared to something else? (the comparison)
- *What* do we wish to occur as a result of our activity? (the outcome)

Three types of outcome questions may be asked: general, specific and comparative, as in Table 2.1.

As questions become more specific, the narrower is the range of information required to answer them, and the tighter the limits we must place on our search. For instance, we might start with a general question in mind, as illustrated in Table 2.2.

Table 2.1   Different types of research questions

General	Specific	Comparative
We know what the problem is, but have no particular solutions in mind.	We know what the problem is, and have a solution in mind, but we want to know whether it works or not.	We know what the problem is, and have several solutions in mind. We want to know which one is likely to be the more effective.
e.g. What works in improving *coping ability* in mothers with po*s*t-natal depression?	e.g. Is counselling effective in improving coping ability in *mothers with post-natal depression?*	e.g. How does *counselling* compare to *peer support* for mothers with post-natal depression?

| | Outcome | Population | Intervention | Comparison |

Table 2.2   General questions

General questions – the outcome is known but not the intervention

How can we safeguard the health of looked after children? (*Outcome – maintenance of good health*)

How can we help adults with learning difficulties find work? (*Outcome – job placement*)

What is the best way of encouraging fathers to attend programmes in family centres? (*Outcome – increased programme attendance*)

Having acquired information about the range of options available, we might look in more depth at an intervention, procedure or strategy in which we have a particular interest, as in Table 2.3.

We might also choose to go further and search for studies which compare the respective merits of different approaches to the same issue; see Table 2.4.

These components of an outcomes research question will become the search terms you employ when creating a search strategy on a database. For example, in Table 2.1 above, depending on how specific you want to be, your search strategy will use some or all of the following terms: 'post-natal

Table 2.3 Specific questions

Specific questions – both the outcome and the intervention are known

---

I am working with a 15-year-old boy who has several convictions for theft and 'taking and driving away'. How likely is it that **a week long outward bound course** (*Intervention*) will successfully divert him from offending behaviour? (*Outcome – reduced offending*)

Can **key worker systems** (*Intervention*) for disabled children and their parents help increase family income? (*Outcome – increase in income*)

Will **reminder phone-calls** (*Intervention*) the day before clients are due to attend family centre programmes reduce programme attrition? (*Outcome – reduction in programme drop-out*)

Table 2.4 Comparative questions

Comparative questions – the problem is defined and a comparison sought between two or more interventions

---

Are **work preparation schemes** (*Intervention*) more effective than **work placement schemes** (*Comparison*) at securing long term employment for adults with learning disabilities? (*Outcome – long-term employment*)

Are **client-held records** (*Intervention*) more effective than **agency-held records** (*Comparison*) in achieving (a) greater user satisfaction with services and (b) greater record accuracy? (*Outcomes – user satisfaction and record accuracy*)

I am discussing a programme of short term breaks for a disabled child. She and her parents want to ensure that she is able to use as many ordinary community facilities as possible. Will a **residential home** (*Intervention*) or a **foster family** (*Intervention*) be more successful at meeting the family's requirements? (*Outcome – use of community facilities*)

---

depression', 'counselling', 'peer support'. Creating a search strategy is discussed in more detail later in the chapter.

As noted above, as well as asking questions about outcomes, you are also likely to want to ask *process questions*. Knowing how effective interventions or approaches are, is of importance, but so too is knowledge about the experiences and views of people using and delivering services. Although these questions can be answered through individual feedback and consultation with

Table 2.5   Process questions

What do *homeless couples* think of the *level and type* of *hostel provision* available to them?

    ↑   ↑   ↑

Population   Process issue = views of service   Intervention

Potential search terms might be: 'couples', 'views', 'experience', 'homeless', 'hostel', 'accommodation'.

Another question might be:

How do *people with schizophrenia* perceive and experience their condition?

             ↑   ↑

        Population   Process issue = experience of a condition

Possible search terms might be: 'schizophrenia', 'experience', 'views', 'perceive', 'perception'.

---

groups of service users or staff, this information can be collected more systematically using qualitative research designs. Gaining knowledge of the meanings attached to wheelchair use by disabled parents, for example, may help us understand more about their support requirements. Finding out what older people want from their home carers can help us avoid mistakes and provide the sort of home help and support that older people really need. Understanding what staff feel works and doesn't work about an inter-agency project can help managers devise how best to configure services. Process questions will have differing components depending on the nature of the question being asked, and instead of an outcome, there will be a *process* issue, as illustrated in Table 2.5.

Whatever the practice problem we are confronted with, we need to reduce the issue to an answerable question. Failure to do so is likely to result in the wrong information being returned, insufficient information or too much information. In each case, someone's time will be wasted and much frustration may result. Only once we have a clear question will we be able to formulate a suitable searching strategy with appropriate search terms. Deciding on whether our question is an outcome or a process question, and recognising which level of information is required will also make the process easier. Once we have done this, we are ready to explore the literature to see what we can find.

Sources of research on social work and social care

It has already been noted that a major problem confronting all professions is how to manage the vast amount of information available in the public realm.

Depending on the knowledge needed, relevant information can be accessed via the following sources: libraries, grey literature, gateways, search engines, statistical collections and journals. The examples highlighted below provide a flavour; more extensive lists can be found in the resources section.

Libraries

Some practitioners may work for authorities or organisations that possess their own libraries or who have arrangements with university libraries. When this is not the case, if a university library is in reach, it is worth checking whether access to the collections is available to the public. This is unlikely to include borrowing rights, but university libraries do usually allow members of the public to access their collections for reference purposes, allowing you to photocopy individual journal articles or book chapters as required. While some may restrict access to holiday periods, this is nonetheless an invaluable service. Additionally, external membership of university libraries is often available for a reasonable fee.

Library staff should also be considered as a crucial resource. They will be highly knowledgeable about not only their own collections, but library holdings in general and are normally (if cultivated politely) eager to meet the knowledge requirements of both students and members of the public. Any individual library is also a window to the full range of both national and international literature, any item of which can be accessed, for a modest fee, through the inter-library loan facility. This is essentially a lending system run by the British Library, which allows any member of the public to borrow material held therein. The British Library holds copies of all published literature in the UK, including journals, and many publications from overseas. If the library does not hold the item you are looking for, staff there will do their utmost to locate it from elsewhere on your behalf. To use inter-library loans, you simply need to fill in a slip held in your local public library or university library, and pay a small charge (currently around £2–3 in public libraries, significantly less than in most university libraries). Alternatively you can order documents directly from the British Library catalogue.[4] Books must be returned but photocopied journal articles are yours to keep. The British Library houses the largest collections of books and journals in the country. Its online catalogue enables the enquirer to search collections held in both its London premises and its depository in Boston Spa, Yorkshire. Joining the British Library is slightly more complicated than other libraries; prospective members are required to submit an application, stating for what purposes they wish to use the library, and providing some form of proof of this, such as a letter from

---

[4] *http://catalogue.bl.uk*

an employer. If access to the British Library at St Pancras in London is a practical option on a regular or occasional basis, information on how to acquire membership is available at their website.[5]

If you do not have time physically to visit a library, further virtual options are available, in that many library catalogues are freely accessible via the internet. Most UK university library catalogues can be accessed directly through the respective university website (the website addresses of UK academic institutions all end in .ac.uk). Many catalogues, such as that of the University of Exeter, contain links to other library catalogues.[6] Accessing COPAC,[7] which covers the collections of the largest academic libraries in Britain, will allow you to carry out simultaneous searches of several university library catalogues, including the British Library.

Public libraries have not progressed, to date, as far as academic libraries in making their collections publicly available on the internet. Those that do have online catalogues can be found on the UK Public Libraries Page,[8] under the section 'Public Library OPACS'.

For all their usefulness, it is important to note that there are a few limitations of library catalogues. For example, they provide listings of books and journal titles rather than individual journal articles (databases fulfil the latter role – see below). While some primary research may be published in book form, books tend to be more useful to the practitioner in giving an overview of a particular issue, or the theoretical background to an area of work. As the publishing schedule of books is often much longer than that of journal articles, their topicality may weaken correspondingly quickly. Furthermore, library catalogues rarely provide summaries of the *content* of books, so it is often difficult to assess the relevance of a volume without actually examining it. The value of library catalogues to most practitioners will primarily be as a locational device, that is, to establish whether a particular item, such as a book or journal series, is held in the collection concerned.

Grey literature

Grey literature has traditionally referred to material that has not reached a commercial publisher and is not fully in the public domain, but was circulated informally or made available to particular groups. In the field of social work, grey literature will most often be represented by reports or evaluations produced or commissioned by local authorities, social welfare organisations

---

[5] *www.bl.uk/*
[6] *www.ex.ac.uk/library/uklibs.html*
[7] *www.copac.ac.uk/copac/*
[8] *http://dspace.dial.pipex.com/town/square/ac940/weblibs.html#opacs*

or charities designed for internal consumption. Grey literature reports can be highly illuminating, as they are often focused on important practice or policy issues and may be more practice-oriented than much of the published academic literature.

Searching systematically for grey literature can be difficult, since catalogues and databases primarily index published literature. However, becoming familiar with a few key resources and websites should be ample for the needs of most practitioners. Checking the publication catalogues of major charities is one simple way of accessing some important grey literature; often reports may be available to download in full. For example, reports produced by Barnardo's are available from the charity's website.[9] Both the Charities Digest and the Voluntary Agencies Directory should be available in main public libraries. These give details of the work of charitable and voluntary organisations, including whether the organisation has a library and information service, or whether it produces reports. Contact details are provided, enabling direct enquiries to be made.

A sample of additional websites containing grey literature aimed at practitioners in social care and allied fields is given in Table 2.6 below (a more comprehensive list is provided in the resource section).

Specialist gateways/directories

If you are searching for additional links but do not know where to look, gateways or directories provide a useful starting point. The basic principle of a gateway is that it provides links to a selection of websites that have been chosen by a subject expert for their relevance and quality. As well as having a links section, gateways often have sections devoted to research, statistics, events and news, and provide access to e-mail lists or discussion groups. Specialist gateways can be found for most academic disciplines and many professions, and are updated fairly regularly by information scientists or librarians. Typically, a gateway will be sorted into categories and sub-categories, allowing you to browse by subject area. Alternatively, they have in-built search engines which can be used for more focused searching.

While the obvious advantage of a specialist gateway is that someone has already done the work for us by locating online resources relevant to our field of work, bear in mind also that the sites selected will reflect the biases and limited knowledge of the person entering the data, and that they may not be completely up to date. For this reason it is always worth keeping an eye on a few different gateways. Examples of gateways relevant to social care are:

---

[9] *www.barnardos.org.uk*

Table 2.6 Sources of grey literature

Organisation	Web address and main area of research	Main features
Joseph Rowntree Foundation	*www.jrf.org.uk* Care and housing	Allows you to search JRF publications, work in progress, responses to government consultations and press releases. Also a useful 'findings' series – short, user-friendly research summaries.
Research in Practice	*www.rip.org.uk* Child care	Research publications produced by RiP on many child care subjects, Quality Protects briefings, and Policy and Research Updates.
Evidence Network	*www.evidencenetwork.org* Broad range of social and health care topics such as child care, public health and neighbourhood research	Links to abstracts and many full text documents of systematic reviews and other publications in social care and health topics. Links to interesting articles on research utilisation and uptake.
What works for Children?	*www.whatworksforchildren. org.uk* Child care	A resources section with research briefings, evidence 'nuggets' and resources to support evidence-based practice.
Mental Health Foundation	*www.mentalhealth.org.uk* Mental health	Some fully downloadable research reports; a listing of all the organisation's publications which can be purchased online; updates, briefings and fact sheets.

- The Social Science Information Gateway: *www.sosig.ac.uk*
- Electronic Library for Social Care: *www.elsc.org.uk/*

The latter gateway is likely to be the one most used by social care staff. Its opening screen looks like Figure 2.1:

Figure 2.1   Electronic Library for Social Care (eLSC)

The following case study is an example of how we might use the eLSC.

Gateways Case Study: the eLSC

You are a senior practitioner in a new multi-agency team that has been established to work with older people with mental health problems. You are interested in finding out what the research says about which interventions are effective and also about the views and experiences of older clients who use mental health services. For a general query such as this, the eLSC is a good starting point, since it is a specialist social care gateway.

The eLSC contains a series of good practice guides, one of which is about assessing the mental health needs of older people. It also provides access to a database of online journals. A search on this using the term 'older people with mental health problems' brings up details of three journals: *Aging & Mental Health*, *The International Journal of Geriatric Psychiatry* and *Dementia: The International Journal of Social Research and Practice*. Descriptions of each of these journals are given along with advice on how to access electronic information about their content. By registering for their e-mail contents alerting service, which you can do at the click of a few buttons, you will be confident that you are keeping up to date with much of the latest research in this field.

The eLSC provides access to AgeInfo, a database specialising in issues relating to older people, run by the Centre for Policy on Ageing. By searching on this database using terms such as 'mental health' and 'views', a list of journals and reports is retrieved, containing summary information about each document.

A search on the 'users and carers' database on the eLSC using the same term brings up 71 references to articles and reports about older people with mental health problems, many of which report studies exploring user views. There is also a database called CareData on the eLSC (described in more detail below). Searching this entire database returns a much larger number of references on the subject.

The key links section allows you to search for websites by client group. Clicking on 'older people' produces a list of 20 websites belonging to charities, research organisations and other information sites. Viewing the 'mental health' list returns you with details of the websites of 16 specialist mental health organisations. These websites may be very good sources of grey literature, as discussed above.

By following the link to the 'be-evidence-based.com' website contained on the eLSC homepage, you can access a summary of critically appraised research relating to older people with dementia, which spells out key findings from several research studies and discusses their practice implications.

Lastly, by clicking on 'events in the social care world', also on the home page, you can access lists of events published by different social care magazines and a national newspaper. Checking this section regularly would be a good way of keeping up to date with any conferences or workshops being run nationally on mental health issues in relation to older people.

A gateway can therefore provide us with numerous types of information: news, events, practice guidance and policy documents as well as research. While gateways are not, generally speaking, the place to obtain *specific* pieces of research, they can certainly be used to access places where research studies can be located. While no practitioner can be expected to keep up to date across the whole spectrum of research in social care, selective searching of electronic resources, and making arrangements to receive information or e-mail alerts of material relevant to one's specialist area, can ensure that we keep up to date on new developments within our specific fields.

Search engines

Search engines can also be a useful way of locating websites that may contain research evidence relevant to social work. Examples are Google,[10] AltaVista,[11] Ask Jeeves[12] and Lycos.[13] Like gateways, search engines are not ideal for locating specific pieces of published research evidence of the type that you would find in journals. Their usefulness lies in their ability to locate websites of interest which may contain relevant grey literature or links to databases which contain published research.

However, due to the broad coverage of search engines as compared to gateways (search engines search the entire World Wide Web rather than a selection of sites), the amount of information they retrieve can be overwhelming. A few simple searching rules and tips can help ensure that your search results are relevant and focused. For instance, on the UK version of the search engine Google,[14] by inserting quotation marks round the phrase "social care journals" the search engine will retrieve only sites that contain that entire phrase (71 such sites on 06/02/04) rather than those which contain all of the words within it but not as a distinct phrase (4,820,000!). On the advanced search screen, you can also apply limits by searching only for this phrase when it appears in the title of the page rather than anywhere in the text of the page. This reduces your results list to only 3, a much more manageable number. Searches can also be refined by language, country and date (such as the past three months, past six months, or past year). Each search engine contains its own help section advising on the best way to combine search terms, and spending five minutes on this section will undoubtedly save you time in the long run.

Statistics

Most practitioners are likely to need basic statistical information about key features of the client group with whom they work. Managers may also need information on trends over time, changing demographic profiles, or the prevalence of conditions within the local or national population. Official statistical data for the UK, including the 2001 Census, may be found on the Office for National Statistics (ONS) website.[15] The material of most interest to social workers can be found in the section 'health and care'. ONS produce an

---

[10] *www.google.com*
[11] *www.altavista.com*
[12] *www.ask.com*
[13] *www.lycos.com*
[14] *www.google.co.uk*
[15] *www.statistics.gov.uk*

indispensable *Guide to Official Statistics*, which tells us where data on a specific topic can be found, what the data consist of, and who to contact for further information. This guide can be accessed online.[16]

The ONS also publishes the *Annual Abstract of Statistics*, which is a compilation of data from a wide range of authoritative sources. Trends over 10 years are presented. Tables are organised by subject and details of the contributing organisation provided. The compendium can be viewed and downloaded from the ONS website.[17]

Most of the data from the 2001 Census data are now available for the whole of the UK, by nation, or by geographical area down to ward level. Census data may be accessed free of charge on the internet.[18] The ONS has a very helpful online enquiry service, which will personally respond to e-mail enquires about official data. This can be reached on: *info@statistics.gov.uk*

Key statistical data relating to both children and adults services in England may be found on the websites of the Department for Education and Skills and the Department of Health.[19] This section largely contains data collected from the statistical returns provided by local authorities to the Department of Health, providing useful overview information about numbers receiving different services as well as trends over time. It also contains analysis of national targets and performance.

Local statistics may often be of more use to the practitioner. These are available through ONS publications such as Regional Trends, Population Trends and Labour Market Trends, again from the ONS website. Many local authorities maintain websites which contain key statistical data for their populations down to town and district level. To check the content of these websites, go first to the main UK government's website,[20] then browse the local government index and click on the appropriate local authority link.

Journals

Journals generally constitute the best source of primary research relevant to the needs of practitioners. They are usually published several times per year, include articles that focus on micro- as well as macro- level issues and usually include an abstract or summary of the key points. Good abstracts would include information about the study design, the main findings and implications. The content of journals varies from those which are best described as trade papers, such as *Community Care or Professional Social Work*, to journals

---

[16] *www.statistics.gov.uk/downloads/theme_compendia/GOS2000_v5.pdf*
[17] *www.statistics.gov.uk/StatBase/Product.asp?vlnk = 94&Pos = &ColRank = 1&Rank = 422*
[18] *www.statistics.gov.uk/census2001/default.asp*
[19] *www.dfes.gov.uk; www.dh.gov.uk*
[20] *www.direct.gov.uk/*

which seek to highlight day to day practice issues, and often include articles written by practitioners, such as *Practice*, to peer-reviewed journals which are the favoured route for academic publishing, such as the *British Journal of Social Work* or the *Journal of Social Work Practice*. Primary research is more likely to be found in peer-reviewed journals (so called because article acceptance is dependent upon a review and approval procedure led by experts in the respective field). Given the extremely broad range of issues addressed by social work and social care staff, practitioners should not be too parochial in their choice of reading – many journals which focus on health, psychology and education contain highly relevant material.

Academics are likely to be familiar with the main journals in their field and have regular access to them. This is not likely to be the situation with practitioners. The best way to identify relevant material is via an electronic database.

Databases

Electronic databases contain references to and usually summaries (or 'abstracts') of individual journal articles. They are the best possible tool for locating primary research, since they scan the contents of large numbers of journals on the subject areas covered by the database. Some also include book chapters, editorials, letters and book reviews. Databases offer some or all of the following features:

- Search facilities that enable us to identify articles using a number of criteria, e.g. author, subject, year of publication.
- Hyperlinks to other associated websites or online material e.g. home pages of journals.
- The full text of articles may be offered online by some individual journals, in some cases for free, but in most cases through either a one-off payment or, for regular access to the journal, by annual subscription. However, many journals which require subscription provide free online access to back copies.
- The facility to select a list of items and to print, download or e-mail to oneself or a colleague.

The following are two typical database items from CareData, the social care database run by the Social Care Institute for Excellence. Key words and phrases are in bold. Both abstracts contain links to the journals' home pages.

As noted above, CareData is available through the electronic Library for Social Care (eLSC) and is the 'first stop' online resource for social work and social care staff. Its disadvantages are that is has a relatively unsophisticated, though easy to use search engine (which is currently being improved and

CLARE Linda, COX Sylvia.
Improving service approaches and outcomes for people with complex needs through consultation and involvement.
Disability and Society , 18(7), December 2003, pp. 935–953.
Link to the Journal home page 2003

Services have not always catered well for people with complex needs. The term 'complex needs' is used here to signify people who have cognitive impairments and communication difficulties that present major challenges for getting one's views and preferences heard and understood, and/or who may not fit into traditional categories of service provision. Current developments in policy and practice, such as the single shared assessment process, emphasise inclusion through user involvement. There is a danger, however, that people with complex needs will be seen as too difficult to involve, and will therefore remain effectively excluded from the decision-making process and from the opportunity to influence service provision. This article explores the current situation in relation to ensuring genuine involvement for people with complex needs, highlights obstacles to progress and examples of good practice, and identifies future directions for research and practice.

Disabled People; People With Learning Difficulties; Communication Disorders; Provision of Services; Policy Formulation; User Involvement; User Views; Unmet Need; Decision Making; Action Research

© **All references on CareData are copyright SCIE**

COWLING Vicki et al.
Children of adults with severe mental illness: mental health, help seeking and service use.
Psychiatric Bulletin, 28(2), February 2004, pp. 43–46.
Link to the Journal home page 2004

Reports on an Australian study to determine the prevalence of childhood mental health problems in children of parents registered with an area mental health service, and to study the parents' help-seeking and service use for their children. Parents were recruited through their case managers, and asked to complete the Strengths and Difficulties Questionnaire (SDQ), the Service Utilisation Questionnaire and the Help-seeking Questionnaire. Results found a quarter of the children were in the clinical range of the SDQ total scores, with high sub-scale scores. However, 63 percent of the parents reported reluctance to seek help, and 19 percent reported not using services. Concludes that children of parents with mental illness are at higher risk of childhood psychiatric disorders. Assessment of the child at the time of referral of the parent is an opportunity for problem identification, parental education, and early intervention.

People With Severe Mental Health Problems; Access to Services; Research; Australia; Children With Mental Health Problems; Risk; Assessment

© **All references on CareData are copyright SCIE**

Figure 2.2 Sample abstracts from CareData (reproduced with the permission of the Social Care Institute for Excellence)

upgraded), its indexing of keywords can be a little eccentric, it is not 'quality controlled' in terms of robustness of information included, and the abstracts vary in their usefulness (some are extremely short). However, it contains not only research reports, but details of books, reports, practice guides and grey literature, covering the full range of issues of concern to social work and social care staff. Another freely available database is PubMed,[21] which although primarily a database focusing on health issues, is useful in that it provides much useful information about the aetiology of different conditions. It will be of particular use to occupational therapists, public health staff, social workers specialising in mental health or disability issues, hospital social workers and indeed anyone coming into contact with people with different health problems. PubMed also includes research on the effectiveness of psychosocial interventions which may be of interest to social workers in relevant fields. Details of both free access and subscription databases relevant to social work and social care is provided in the resources section.

For comprehensive searches, for example when undertaking a literature review, we may need to search systematically across a number of databases, since each one may specialise in a slightly different subject area and cover a different range of journals. However, practitioners are extremely busy people and may rightly feel they have more important jobs to do. Therefore if a library service is available in your department, it is strongly advised that you consult a librarian or other information professional for advice. Nevertheless, you may sometimes only need to identify two or three key papers in order to get started on a subject, and in this situation it is extremely valuable to have some basic database searching skills.

Basic techniques for searching databases

As discussed above, the best approach for anyone wishing to formulate a simple search strategy is to generate key words or concepts derived from their search question. Questions will be broken down into phrases and phrases into words. These are often referred to as 'search terms'. The search engine of the database will scan the title and/or abstract for these terms, depending on which option is selected.

---

[21] *www.pubmed.com*

An example

Search question: *How effective are work placements for people with mental health problems as a route to permanent employment?*

Key concepts in the phrase:
Subject: *people with mental health problems*
Topic: *work*
Outcome: *permanent employment*

Search terms: 'work', 'mental health', 'employment'.

We will also want to consider using other associated terms, 'training', 'placement', 'vocation', 'job', 'mental illness', 'mentally ill'. This is particularly important if we are searching international literature, where different terminology may be used.

Databases allow their content to be searched in two ways; either by key words, which have been catalogued as such and are recognised by the programme, or by free text, where we are able to insert whatever terms we think are relevant. CareData is an example of the former, PubMed an example of the latter. Every database has its own conventions for searching and time spent becoming acquainted with their specific idiosyncrasies is well worth it. Always therefore check the help section of a new database. Nonetheless, there are a few simple search rules that most database search engines have in common.

Search engines enable us to connect terms using joining words or symbols. These are known as Boolean operators – AND, OR and NOT (on CareData the symbols & / ! respectively are used instead). For example, connecting the words with AND (**work AND mental health**) will only locate items which feature *both* terms. The term AND, therefore, narrows our search. Connecting the words with OR (**work OR mental health**) will locate items that contain *either* term, broadening our search. Searching with the term NOT will narrow the search, so **work NOT mental health** will return all items that concern work *except* those that feature mental health. However, caution should be exercised when using the NOT operator; by excluding a certain category of material, we could easily inadvertently miss some documents that have useful information on the topic we are researching. For example, **work NOT mental health** may be a helpful search phrase if we are interested in employment but not interested in mental health aspects of it such as stress or depression; however, we may inadvertently exclude relevant research on those working in the mental health sector.

Another important operator is the truncation or wildcard. This is a symbol, usually an asterisk, which substitutes for a suffix. For example, **child*** will locate records that contain the word child, but also children; **therap*** will locate therapy and therapeutic; **depress*** will find depression and depressive, and so on. Asterisks can often also be used as a prefix; ***abuse**, for example, would locate child abuse, elder abuse and financial abuse. Some databases use the dollar sign (e.g child$) instead of an asterisk. Many databases allow us to use 'variant spelling', which would locate different spellings of the same word, e.g. organisation, and organization. A question mark is often used for this, i.e. **organi?ation**. The help page of a database will advise on the appropriate truncation symbol.

Phrasing is also a valuable strategy. This means an entire phrase rather than individual terms are located. For example, **"community care"** would ensure that items which contain this phrase, rather than the words 'community' and 'care' separately are returned. This is an important searching tool not only for databases but also for general search engines such as Google.

Advanced techniques for database searching

For more complex searches, many databases allow us to use parentheses to structure our search. Using brackets allows us to group terms and avoid ambiguity. For example, **"social work" AND (evidence OR research)** will search for documents containing either *evidence* and social work, or *research* and social work. A more complicated search string might look like this: **("social work" AND (evidence OR research)) NOT case study**. The technique whereby one parenthesis is used inside another is referred to as 'nesting'. 'Proximity searching' is another way of narrowing a search. This enables us to retrieve key words within a certain distance of each other. Different databases use different proximity operators. Web of Science,[22] for instance (a database covering science, social science and health topics), uses the word 'same' – e.g. the phrase **"social work" same research**, retrieves records where the two key words appear in the same sentence. Others use the word 'near' to achieve a similar thing. **"Social work" near evidence** will locate records where the two keywords appear no more than 10 words apart. These advanced searching techniques are rarely needed but they are worthwhile knowing about for those times when our basic searching does not seem to be finding what we are looking for.

Refining your search

Having conducted our initial database search, we may find that we have a) too little information, or b) too much information. In either case, we may have to come up with alternative search terms related to our original ones, as in the example above of work, employment, job and so on.

---

[22] *www.isinet.com/products/citation/wos/*

When you have too little information

In scenario *a*, when we have too *little* information, we may have to broaden our search by using the OR operator described above. Alternatively, it may be that there is very little research out there on the subject in which we are interested, particularly if it is an emerging field. We will have to think laterally: is there research on related fields or topics that might still be relevant? For example, there may not be much research on increasing 'service user involvement' amongst children who have been abused, yet there is an extensive literature on involving children generally in service development, which may be of use. Or, while we may not be able to find specific information about effective approaches to supported accommodation for people with Asperger's Syndrome, we may find relevant research on supported accommodation for people with learning difficulties generally. This is a common problem encountered by practitioners new to searching, who may be attempting to look for highly specific information that simply does not exist. While it is always wise to be careful not to make *assumptions* about the transferability of research from one field or one client group to another, it is also unrealistic to assume that the research we want will always be available. When there really is no research to support or back an intervention, we must exercise caution in our use of it and retain an open mind about alternatives. Alternatively, we may wish to conduct our own local evaluation to measure the effectiveness of the intervention in question (conducting evaluations is discussed in Chapter 6).

When you have too much information

In scenario *b* when we have too *much* information, we may have to limit our search using AND or NOT. Alternatively, we may wish to limit our search by language, date or study type (e.g. only systematic reviews or randomised controlled trials). Most databases provide these 'limiters'. In a well-researched field we may have the luxury of choosing between many studies, in which case we should choose the best available research. By best, we mean research which is well-conducted and which uses bias-reducing methodologies. This is discussed more fully in the next chapter.

A note on limiting searches: sensitivity and specificity

So we now know that databases enable the user, with differing degrees of sophistication, to place limits on a search. The purpose of limiting a search is to locate the largest number of relevant results while minimising the irrelevant ones. Different databases vary in their ability to deliver the maximum number of 'hits' and the minimum number of 'misses'. These two dimensions are referred to as sensitivity and specificity.

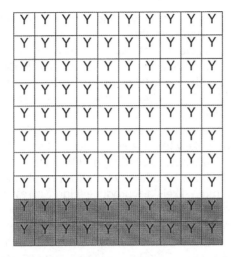

Figure 2.3   Sensitivity and specificity

Sensitivity describes the proportion of relevant items which are located by a search. While all searches need high sensitivity, this dimension alone is insufficient. We must also strive for high *specificity*, which is an expression of the ratio between 'hits' and 'misses'. The importance of this should not be underestimated. A search with low sensitivity will simply not return the information we need, or worse, will return incomplete information leading us to make erroneous conclusions. A search with low specificity may return many hundreds, or even thousands, of items, most of which will be irrelevant, but which will all have to be examined before being discarded – often a very lengthy and arduous task. As we are unlikely to know the total number of relevant items in the 'universe' which we are examining in advance, we measure the sensitivity and specificity of a particular database by comparing it with the combined performance of all relevant databases. For example, we might be interested in interventions which aim to improve the educational attainments of looked after girls.

In Figure 2.3 the 100 cells represent all known studies on the educational attainment of looked after children. Y is a relevant result, N an irrelevant one. The grey cells (n = 20) represent true positives, that is, items specifically concerning looked after females. The white cells (n = 80) represent false positives, that is, items which are not specifically concerned with girls.

We can calculate sensitivity by dividing the total number of items located that match the search criteria by the total number of known items. The search has achieved high sensitivity by the simple expedient of locating every known study on the educational attainment of looked after children, regardless of whether they concern girls or boys. The sensitivity of this search is thus 20/20 = 100 per cent. However, the precision – specificity – of the search is also important to us, as we do not want to waste time reading through and discarding irrelevant items. Specificity is measured by dividing the *number of relevant articles* located by the *total number* of items found. The specificity of this search is thus 20/100 = 20 per cent. If we had been more careful with our search criteria, by ensuring that only studies relating to looked after *girls* were located, we could have improved the degree of our specificity.

No search strategy is likely to achieve 100 per cent sensitivity and specificity. However, different databases, depending on the subject, vary in their degree of sensitivity and specificity, and it may help for practitioners to be aware of the ones that are more likely to produce high scores in their particular speciality. For example, in relation to decision making on care options for elderly people, CareData achieves a sensitivity of only one per cent, that is, returns only 1/100 of the total number of relevant items, compared to 41 per cent by Medline. However, CareData achieves a specificity of 94 per cent. While missing a large number of relevant studies, almost all the ones it did identify were relevant – a much better performance on this dimension than Medline, which only managed 48 per cent [6]. This highlights the importance of conducting searches across several databases, as relying on a single source of information will undoubtedly lead to large numbers of relevant items being missed. Putting limits on a search inevitably compromises its sensitivity but, where a very large body of information exists, the greater specificity achieved will often be worth it. For example, the search profile in Figure 2.4 will probably be of more use to us than that illustrated in Figure 2.3, despite its lower sensitivity.

This search has located 16/20 of the relevant studies and thus has a sensitivity of 80 per cent. It has also located 16 studies that were not relevant, hence its specificity is 16/32 = 50 per cent. Or to quantify it in terms of time, if it takes us two minutes to examine an item and decide whether it is relevant or not, the profile in Figure 2.3 will require almost three and a half hours of reading to identify 20 relevant items, while we can locate 16 from just over one hour of reading in the Figure 2.4 profile – a good trade off for most busy professionals.

Librarians are an excellent source of advice as to which database is most likely to satisfy your information needs.

Some worked examples of database searches

Some typical social care database searches are provided below. These are drawn from non-subscription databases available to anyone with access to the internet.

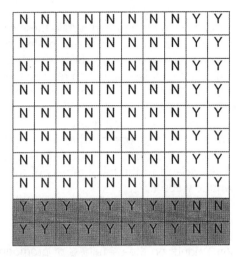

Figure 2.4   A typical search profile

Example 1

A project for young offenders has always considered the promotion of self-esteem to be an important element in the programme. A number of programme activities specifically set out to improve self-esteem. You are a new team leader reviewing the core elements of the programme. While a belief that low self-esteem is associated with offending behaviour is widespread among members of your team, and is supported by many anecdotes, nobody in the team can actually cite any strong evidence base for this belief. You decide to search CareData:

1. Log onto *www.elsc.org.uk*
2. Click on the CareData button
3. Click search CareData
4. You begin with a broad search. Check that you are using the right keyword by clicking on the letter 'S' below the keyword field. Scroll down and you will find 'self esteem'. Return to the search screen and type **self esteem** in the keyword field (you can also cut and paste the term from the keyword field).
5. As you are interested in more recent studies, you decide to confine your search to publications later than 2000.
6. Enter date preceded by 'greater than' symbol – >2000 – in the year field.
7. Click 'submit query'.

8. You will find 229 abstracts returned. While these can be browsed through, you are pressed for time and prefer to narrow your search. You know that examining publications that review lots of different studies takes far less time than reading them all yourself.
9. Click on letter 'R'. The keyword you need is 'reviews'.
10. Add the symbol for 'and' – & – after 'self esteem' and type or cut and paste 'reviews'. Click 'submit query'.
11. Seven records are returned, one of which is a review of the costs and causes of low self esteem by Nicholas Emler, dated 2001 [7]. A direct link is available to the full summary of the review on the Joseph Rowntree website.[23]
[Search conducted 07/02/04]

This review casts some doubt on the usefulness of promoting self-esteem as a solution to certain child care problems. It suggests that self-esteem will only tend to emerge once competencies have been developed. You begin a dialogue with your colleagues as to how your programme can start to shift its balance towards helping young people acquire useful and valued skills.

Example 2

You are involved in a setting up a community outreach service which is being established to deal specifically with the increasing numbers of people in your locality presenting with both mental health and substance abuse problems. You know that assertive outreach is the most common approach to this sort of work, but want to find out exactly what the research evidence there is about this. You decide to search PubMed.
1. Click on *www.pubmed.com*
2. Type **assertive outreach** and click on 'GO'.
3. You will find 54 records returned, too many to read in the time you have available, and many irrelevant.
4. Add **AND substance** to your search
5. This time you are presented with only eight records.
6. Two of these are relevant reviews dealing with effective interventions for dual diagnosis.
[Search conducted 07/02/04]

---

[23] *www.jrf.org.uk*

The most recent review [8] is about implementing dual diagnosis services for clients with severe mental illness and substance addictions. It suggests that critical components of effective programmes include a comprehensive, long term, staged approach to recovery; assertive outreach; motivational interventions; provision of help to clients in acquiring skills and supports to manage both illnesses and to pursue functional goals; and cultural sensitivity and competence. As well as giving evidence for the effectiveness of assertive outreach, it provides you with further ideas about issues surrounding motivation and goal-setting, and suggests strategies for overcoming barriers to the implementation of dual diagnosis programmes which may help you in setting up this new service.

Example 3

You are a social worker in a multi-disciplinary CAMHS team. You are increasingly encountering children, sometimes of primary school age, who are being prescribed medication, frequently stimulants like Ritalin, for behavioural problems, particularly attention deficit hyperactivity disorder (ADHD). Many of your social work colleagues are unhappy about this practice. Prescribing clinicians tend to be more positive. Parents have mixed views. You know little about the opinions of the children themselves. Most of the material you read and the accounts you hear are based on personal experience, with people tending to be strongly pro- or anti-medication. This is valuable, but you want a more fully rounded viewpoint. You decide to allocate a morning of your time to briefing yourself on ADHD, its diagnosis and treatment, and the general arguments surrounding the subject. You know the British Medical Journal has full text on-line of all its editions, so you decide to start here.

1. Log onto the British Medical Journal at *www.bmj.com*
2. Click on search/archive.
3. Type **attention deficit hyperactivity disorder** in the text/abstract/ title field. Click 'search'. This returns 107 items, too many to scan through.
4. You decide to limit the search by just looking for recent articles, focusing on reviews and not bothering with 'rapid replies'.
5. Add **AND review** to your search string. Check the 'articles only' field (this excludes features such as letters or book reviews and locates only journal articles). Limit the years by searching from February 2001 to February 2004 only, using the drop down boxes. Click 'search'.

6. This search returns 13 articles. The first is a clinical review entitled 'Evidence based paediatrics: Evidence based management of attention deficit hyperactivity disorder' by Guevara and Stein (2001) [9]. It contains the information you need.
[Search conducted 07/02/04]

This article consists of a case study, describing how a doctor searches for information, diagnoses and treats a child who has been referred as possibly being affected by ADHD. The diagnostic criteria for ADHD are given, plus population prevalence, symptoms, co-morbid conditions, a review of the most effective treatments and some discussion of the controversy that surrounds the condition. There are large numbers of online links to other sites and studies on ADHD. You learn that boys are affected three times more often than girls, a third of these children have other disorders and up to half of affected children may still have symptoms in young adulthood. While combined stimulant medication and behavioural therapies appear to have the best results, controversy remains as to whether ADHD is a valid 'condition' or whether it is just at the extreme end of a behavioural continuum. You now feel much more knowledgeable about ADHD, but remain concerned about the lack of information in the literature about the condition from the young person's point of view. You may therefore decide to conduct a database search, using a phrase such as **ADHD AND children AND (views OR opinions)**. If your database searching yields nothing relevant, you might also seek out grey literature from organisations and charities working in this field, as these are unlikely to be indexed on standard databases. You may also wish to consider conducting a piece of qualitative research within your department, exploring the views of children with this condition.

As illustrated in these examples, robust reviews are generally the most helpful source of information for managers and practitioners, especially if they are systematic reviews or meta-analyses. While reviews of these types do not exist in many important subjects in social care, reviews that are clear about their inclusion and exclusion criteria are generally (but not always!) more reliable.

Conclusion

If we have achieved one thing in this chapter we hope it has been to highlight to the reader the wealth of research information that can now be accessed by the social care practitioner, particularly through the internet. We also hope we have demonstrated why it is important, and how it can help, to consider your search question carefully, and break it up into component parts which can then become your search terms. Searching databases and other online resources is not as complicated as people might fear, although there are sophisticated techniques available for those who have had some practice. This chapter has described the key types of resource for locating social care research and introduced some of the most popular freely available examples of these. Those wanting more comprehensive information should consult the Resources section; however, we hope to have illustrated that with access to a modem and a PC, the willingness to spend some time considering a question important to our work, and most of all, a degree of curiosity, we can significantly add to our existing knowledge base.

References

[1] Booth, S.H., Booth, A. and Falzon, L.J. (2003) The need for information and research skills training to support evidence-based social care: a literature review and survey. *Learning in Health and Social Care.* 2: 4, 191–201.

[2] Howard, M.O., McMillen C.J. and Pollio, D.E. (2003) Teaching evidence-based practice: towards a new paradigm for social work education. *Research on Social Work Practice.* 13: 2, 234–59.

[3] Tierney, S. (2002) Reframing an evidence-based approach to practice. *Social Work and Social Sciences Review.* 10: 2, 49–62.

[4] Moseley, A. (2004) The internet: can you get away without it? supporting the caring professions in accessing research for practice. *Journal of Integrated Care.* 12: 3, 30–7.

[5] Sheldon, B., Chilvers, R., Ellis, A., Moseley, A. and Tierney, S. (2004) A pre-post empirical study of obstacles to, and opportunities for, evidence-based practice in social care. In Bilson, A. (Ed.) *Evidence-based Practice and Social Work: International Research and Policy Perspectives.* London: Whiting and Birch.

[6] Taylor, B.J., Dempster, M. and Donnelly, M. (2003) Hidden gems: systematically searching electronic databases for research publications for social work and social care. *British Journal of Social Work.* 33, 423–39.

[7] Emler, N. (2001) *The Costs and Causes of Low Self-esteem.* York: Joseph Rowntree Foundation.

[8] Drake, R.E., Essock, S.M., Shaner, A., Carey, K.B., Minkoff, K., Kola, L., Lynde, D., Osher, F.C., Clark, R.E. and Rickards, L. (2001) Implementing dual diagnosis services for clients with severe mental illness. *Psychiatric Services.* 52: 4, 469–76.

[9] Guevara, J.P. and Stein, M.T. (2001) Evidence based management of attention deficit hyperactivity disorder. *British Medical Journal.* 323, 1232–5.

Chapter 3

Critical Appraisal: Sorting the Wheat From the Chaff

The aims of this chapter are to:
- Explain critical appraisal skills and why social workers need them.
- Introduce the concepts of bias and trustworthiness in research studies.
- Describe what is meant by quantitative and qualitative research.
- Demonstrate the type of questions that can be answered with quantitative and qualitative research methods, and illustrate how these two types of research are complementary.
- Describe *levels of quantitative research evidence*, and explain how these levels enable us to have more or less confidence in research findings.

Don't just do something, sit there.
(Brian Sheldon, personal communication).

What is 'critical appraisal'?

Critical appraisal is about deciding whether or not to use particular research findings to inform decision making within practice. It involves assessing the quality of research reports and judging the extent to which any flaws might affect the study results. It is then possible to weigh up whether the findings reported are strong (or trustworthy) enough to warrant altering current practice [1].

What are critical appraisal skills?

Critical appraisal skills are not simply a set of techniques that can be worked through and ticked off to get a definitive answer about the trustworthiness of a piece of research (although there are guidance tools to help practitioners: see below). Rather, critical appraisal skills are about taking a questioning and considered approach to research reports. This means assessing research with a critical eye and not simply accepting the conclusions as written.

The critically appraising social worker routinely asks: 'Is this research trustworthy enough that I feel comfortable using it to inform my practice decision making?' This involves examining the research for potential bias, and considering how this might impact on the results reported.

Bias and trustworthiness

Bias has been defined as: 'The deviation of results from the truth due to systematic error(s) in the methods used' [2]. Bias can be introduced in to a research study at a number of points, for example, in how the research is conducted, how the data are recorded, or how the information is analysed.

Checking research studies for biases, and considering what influence these are likely to have had on study findings, lies at the heart of critical appraisal. Research is more trustworthy, that is, the findings are more likely to be 'true' and not due to other influences, when bias is kept to a minimum. If a research study is seriously biased you would not want to use its findings in client, practice, or policy decision making because, put frankly, the results and subsequent conclusions could be wrong.

In this chapter we will describe the main types of research study design that social workers are likely to encounter, illustrate these by reference to studies that have been conducted, and detail the types of bias that may affect the trustworthiness of each of these project designs. The relevance of this to social work practice will be demonstrated by reference to two case studies:

Case study 1: Joshua

Joshua is six years old. He lives at home with his mother, two younger brothers and sister. Over the last six months Joshua's mother and his teacher have noticed an increase in anti-social behaviour, manifested by aggression towards other children and an inability to play in groups without causing disruption. This is causing trouble at school and Joshua's mother is finding it difficult to cope with him and her three other children who are all aged five or under. Social services are in contact with Joshua and his family. The family's social worker has heard about a programme being run nearby for children with behavioural problems. The intervention lasts six months, is multi-disciplinary, and is based on the principles of cognitive-behavioural therapy. The social worker wonders whether this would be something that could help Joshua and his family.

Case study 2: Mrs Patel

Mrs Patel is 82 years old and lives at home with her husband. She is currently in hospital, having fractured the neck of her femur after falling at home. She is now medically stable and the hospital is ready to discharge her. Mrs Patel is referred to a social worker, who visits her in hospital. There is a rehabilitation unit nearby, which offers a six-week intermediate care service for older people. The social worker considers whether this would be a good idea for Mrs Patel, or whether she would be better going straight home from hospital. On the basis of the assessment of Mrs Patel's needs and those of her nearest carer, it seems that either option would be appropriate.

We will be referring to these cases throughout the chapter, which looks at both quantitative and qualitative research designs.

Types of research: quantitative and qualitative

There are two broad approaches to research: quantitative and qualitative. The former often focuses on investigations about the effectiveness of services or interventions, such as answering questions about 'what works'. *Outcomes* are considered by counting or measuring, for example in terms of quality of life, educational attainment, prevention of re-offending, or degree of independence. Qualitative research tends to concentrate on understanding meanings, perceptions, experiences and situations.

We see the two methods as complementary. They can give answers to different types of question in the same field. For example, quantitative research could answer the question: *Is cognitive-behavioural therapy more effective than usual care in treating post-natal depression in young, single mothers?* Whereas, qualitative research could answer: *What are the views of young, single mothers with post-natal depression about cognitive-behavioural therapy?*

Types of study design

Quantitative and qualitative research methods include different types of study designs. The main forms used for social care research are shown in Figure 3.1. In the following section we will describe each of these designs, as well as highlighting their strengths and weaknesses and potential sources of bias.

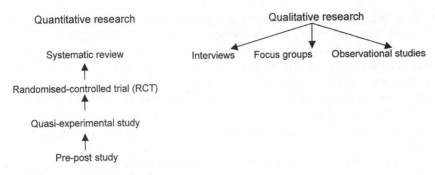

Figure 3.1 Types of research design

Quantitative research: levels of evidence

The different types of quantitative research design to be discussed here are shown in Figure 3.1 as a series of levels. As you go up the levels, the study results are more likely to be trustworthy (if the study has been carried out well) because you can be more certain that any demonstrated effect is due to the intervention itself and not other influences. For example, a study of a behavioural programme designed to reduce the challenging behaviour of primary age children might come to the conclusion that the programme is effective. If this conclusion was drawn from a research study design high in the levels of evidence, we can be much more certain that it was in fact the programme that was responsible for a change in children's behaviour. In contrast, as will be discussed below, if this information was drawn from a study lower in the levels of evidence we cannot be as certain that it was the programme, rather than other influences, that led to an improvement in the youngsters' behaviour.

Pre-post study

The first study design in these levels of evidence is the pre-post study.

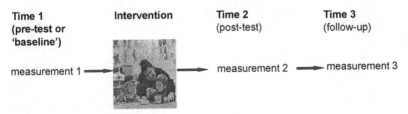

Figure 3.2 Pre-post study

This research design takes a group of individuals and assesses them on one or more measures before an intervention is provided (baseline or time 1) and again when the intervention has finished (time 2), to determine whether there has been a change on the measures from time 1 to time 2. Some pre-post studies also include a follow-up assessment, which is taken at a specific time after the intervention has finished (e.g. six months on). At this point the researchers will measure the same individuals, on the same outcomes, to assess whether any changes found at time 2 have remained, improved, or got worse.

An example of a pre-post study that might have been read by the social worker responsible for Joshua and his family is the *Scallywags* project [3]. This study involved the examination of an intervention to assist families with a child between the ages of two and seven exhibiting behavioural problems. The intervention was based on a multidisciplinary approach. It was a structured, intensive, six month programme, with a strong cognitive-behavioural element, consisting of: assessment, planning and review meetings, an individual child programme, work in the home and pre-school setting, liaison with other services as needed, a local 12 week parenting skills class, and a support group. At the end of the intervention, and at six months follow-up, the children's behaviour had improved (compared to baseline) and parents' levels of stress had decreased (see Figure 3.3).

Findings from this study could be used to inform decision making about service provision for Joshua and his family (Scenario 1). This would mean that any decision was based on a *demonstration* that this type of intervention appears to be effective, rather than a *general impression* that it might help. Hence, the decision to refer Joshua would be based on: 'It has been *shown* to work', rather than, 'we *think* it works'.

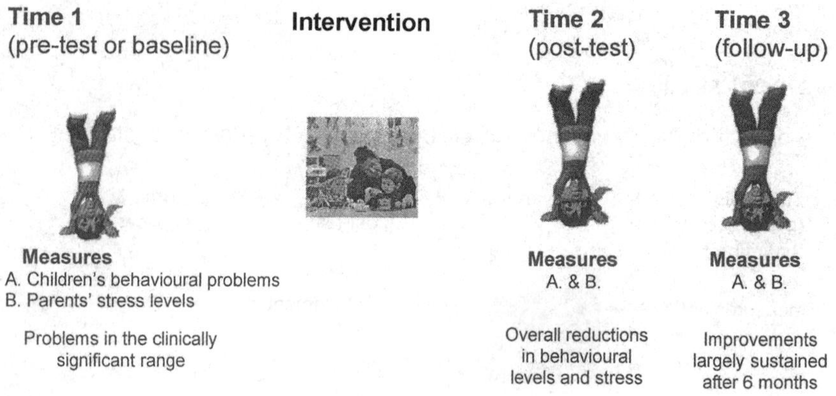

Time 1 (pre-test or baseline)	**Intervention**	**Time 2** (post-test)	**Time 3** (follow-up)

Measures A. Children's behavioural problems B. Parents' stress levels		**Measures** A. & B.	**Measures** A. & B.
Problems in the clinically significant range		Overall reductions in behavioural levels and stress	Improvements largely sustained after 6 months

Figure 3.3   Scallywags project, Cornwall

However, pre-post studies have a design flaw. From the pre-post study described above it *appears* that the intervention is effective. However, the positive results may have been found for a number of other reasons, including:

- The *Hawthorne effect*. This relates to the fact that, generally speaking, if people know they are being observed or assessed, the way in which their performance, behaviour or illness manifests itself may change. This was first noted in the Hawthorne plant of the Western Electric company in the USA. When the company's management started to take an interest in improving production, production increased. This was not as a consequence of actual changes in working conditions introduced by the plant's management, but rather because the management had demonstrated an interest in such improvements. In a research study, people who know they are being 'measured' in some way may 'talk up' their improvements or actually improve *because they are being assessed* rather than because of a specific intervention being provided.
- The *passage of time*. The children's behaviour may have improved anyway six months on, regardless of receiving the intervention or not.
- *Other influences*. There could have been all manner of other changes in the children's lives that resulted in this positive effect on their behaviour. For example, family circumstances at home may have altered, children may have made new friends at school, or no longer been friendly with children who were reinforcing their poor behaviour and so on.

Pre-post studies leave uncertainty about whether it really was the service under investigation that was responsible for any change in the area being measured. This degree of uncertainty is reduced by the next research design up in the levels of evidence; the quasi-experimental study.

Quasi-experimental studies

This research design is set apart from pre-post studies by virtue of the fact that it includes a *comparison* or *control group*. A control group is a sample of people 'matched' to those in the *intervention group* who do not receive the intervention or service whilst the research is underway, but who are also assessed at baseline and at the end of treatment. The structure of quasi-experimental studies is shown in Figure 3.4.

The *Buying Time* project [4] is a quasi-experimental study that might have been read by the social worker responsible for the care of Mrs Patel. The research was funded by the Centre for Evidence-Based Social Services and the NHS Executive South West. Its aim was to determine whether a short stay in a joint social care/health residential rehabilitation unit was more effective for older people being discharged from hospital than going straight home. The study was designed as follows:

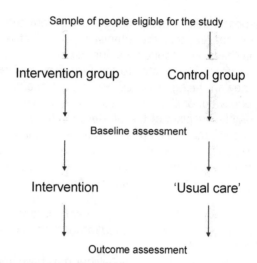

Figure 3.4   Quasi-experimental studies

- Community care workers and occupational therapists referred eligible people to the research team. (Eligibility was over 55 years old, currently in one of ten community hospitals, and likely to benefit from a short-term programme of rehabilitation.)
- The researchers visited all participants whilst they were still in hospital. They were interviewed about their current quality of life – the *baseline assessment.*
- Half of the 200 people interviewed lived in an area that had a residential rehabilitation unit, and they went on to this unit from hospital – the *intervention group.* The other half did not have access to a unit and went straight home from hospital with the usual care they would have ordinarily received – the *control group.*
- As far as was possible, all participants were re-interviewed six and 12 months later to determine whether their quality of life had improved.

The design of the study is shown in Figure 3.5.

The aim of a quasi-experimental study is to determine whether those who receive the intervention *improve more* than those who do not. The *Buying Time* researchers assessed quality of life scores at six and 12 months to determine whether the quality of life of those who went to the unit had *improved more* than that of those who went straight home from hospital. Figure 3.6 shows the findings from baseline (before participants went to the unit or home) to six-month follow-up.

Average quality of life scores for the two groups (intervention and control) at baseline and six-month follow-up are shown in this Figure. A higher quality

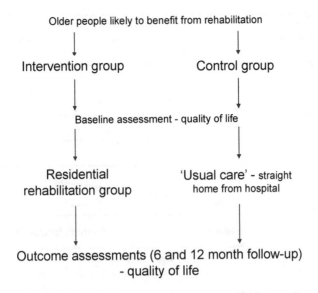

Figure 3.5   The 'Buying Time' study

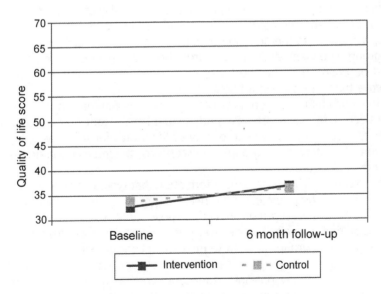

Figure 3.6   Quality of life scores – 'Buying Time' study

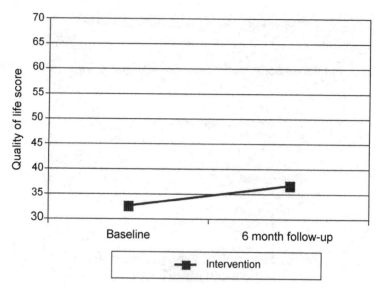

Figure 3.7 Quality of life scores – 'Buying Time' intervention group

of life score indicates a better quality of life. The quality of life scores of *both* groups improved from baseline to six-month follow-up, but the scores of the group who went to the unit did not improve significantly more than those of the group who went straight home from hospital. Therefore, the conclusion could be drawn that the short stay in the rehabilitation unit was *no more effective* than going straight home.

If this study had been conducted as a pre-post design the conclusion would have been different. A pre-post study would have meant no control group, so there would have only been quality of life scores for those who went to the unit (the intervention group). The scores for the intervention group only are shown in Figure 3.7.

This graph, which presents the information that would have been available if the *Buying Time* project had been a pre-post rather than a quasi-experimental study, suggests that a pre-post study would have led to the conclusion that the unit *was* effective. This example demonstrates that studies lacking a control group can lead to misleading conclusions.

Social workers searching for research to aid their decision making are likely to come across many pre-post studies, as compared to the more robust design of quasi-experimental investigations. There are two main reasons for this:

- *Time and money.* Pre-post studies are, on the whole, straightforward and inexpensive to conduct. Often the information needed to make the before-and-after comparisons is already being collected in routine practice or, if it is not, it is not too onerous to gather. Quasi-experimental studies are more time consuming and labour intensive. Time and effort is needed to form a control group and to monitor and assess them in addition to the intervention group. However, the extra time and effort is warranted in order to avoid inaccurate conclusions.

- *Misguided ethics.* An ethical argument is sometimes made for not having a control group. Practitioners may be of the view that it is unethical to deny a new service to people who they think are likely to benefit from it. But the crucial issue here is that at this point the practitioners only *think* their clients will benefit from the new service. It is not until a quasi-experimental study has been conducted that they will have *demonstrated* the effectiveness (or ineffectiveness) of the service over and above ordinary or alternative interventions. Therefore, it can be claimed that it is unethical to provide a service to a large number of people until its effectiveness has been clearly demonstrated. Indeed, it has been argued that practitioners have an ethical obligation to make clear to service users what is known, and not known, about the effectiveness of interventions they suggest [5]. Only then can individuals give their fully informed consent to receive such a service.

At this point, Mrs Patel's social worker (in Scenario 2) might decide that the quasi-experimental *Buying Time* study is a trustworthy source that would prove useful in helping Mrs Patel consider which care pathway she wishes to take. However, before deciding this, the social worker would be wise to check whether the intervention and control groups in the study are *well matched*. In addition, she should consider the potential for *assessor bias*.

In terms of the groups being matched, if intervention and control groups are not similar on key characteristics at baseline, any differences found at follow-up could just be due to these initial differences. In the *Buying Time* study, the researchers took pains to ensure that the characteristics of the two groups involved were as similar as possible at baseline. For example, they had a comparable range of reasons for being admitted to hospital, there were similar proportions of men and women in each group, and so on.

As noted above, *assessor bias* is another issue that can affect the findings of research studies. For example, a project might investigate the effectiveness of body image therapy for young women with anorexia nervosa. Body image in both an intervention group (those who receive body image therapy) and a control group (those who receive usual care only) could be assessed at baseline and then again at the end of the intervention. If the therapists who provided the intervention were also making the body image assessments, it is easy to see how bias could be introduced. The therapists might under-emphasise negative body image in the women who had the body image therapy and over-emphasise it in those who had usual care. This may be easily done, even as an unconscious act; if someone believes in the effectiveness of an intervention or service it is likely that their mindset will favour it.

There is a safeguard that can prevent such assessor bias from occurring. This is to have the person making the assessment of outcomes 'blind' (apologies for this term, but it is routinely used in research reports) to group allocation, that is, when they interview a study participant they do not know whether they are in the intervention or the control group. Research has shown that having an assessor who is *not* 'blind' can lead to biased findings, often with the intervention appearing to be more effective than it actually is.

Mrs Patel's social worker might now have a preference for a quasi-experimental study with well-matched intervention and control groups and 'blind' assessors. However, there is another project design which would give even more trustworthy results.

Randomised controlled trials (RCTs)

Even if researchers try hard to make sure that intervention and control groups in a quasi-experimental study are similar (or 'matched') on what appear to be important characteristics, there may still be key differences on factors that they have not taken note of, recorded, or even thought about. This, again, could mean that differences between groups are found at the end of a study purely because the groups were different at the beginning. This can be overcome by *randomly allocating* participants to the intervention or control group, as illustrated in Figure 3.8.

Going back to Joshua and his family, imagine a study established to investigate the effectiveness of a multi-disciplinary, cognitive-behavioural programme for reducing children's behaviour problems. The degree of behaviour problems of all the children was assessed at baseline. Half of the children were then *randomly allocated* (by the roll of a die or random number tables) to receive the programme (the intervention) or to have the services they would ordinarily receive (the control). After the intervention, the behaviour of all the children was reassessed. The researchers determined whether the behaviour problems of those children who received the programme had improved *more* than the behaviour problems of those who had received ordinary services.

Randomising people to an intervention or control group means that any differences between groups at the outset (or baseline) are due to chance. This minimises the possibility that the groups are *systematically* different in important ways at the start, for example one group being older than the other, or one group having more women or girls than the other. It is assumed that through randomisation all factors that might have an impact on

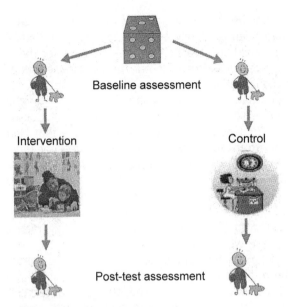

Figure 3.8   Randomised controlled trial

outcomes will be evenly distributed across groups. Because of this, randomised controlled trials are viewed as the highest form of *primary* research design for addressing effectiveness questions [6], where 'primary' refers to individual or single studies (we will discuss secondary research later on in this chapter).

However, even RCTs can be prone to bias if they are poorly conducted. The Lanarkshire milk trial [7] clearly demonstrates how bias can creep into research and affect the trustworthiness of the conclusions drawn. In 1971, Margaret Thatcher, then Secretary of State for Education, was dubbed 'Thatcher the milk snatcher'. This was because the then Conservative government withdrew free school milk for the over sevens (except for under 12s with a medical certificate). The government partly justified this decision by reference to a large research project that had been conducted in the 1930s, which appeared to suggest that giving primary school age children extra milk had no effect on their height or weight.

The Lanarkshire milk experiment took place over four months. Ten thousand children got three-quarters of a pint of milk per day (the intervention group) and an additional 10,000 did not (the control group). At the end of the study, the surprise finding was that the controls were consistently heavier and taller than the children who had the extra milk. It was only years later that the details of how the research had been carried out were considered in detail [8]. This examination showed that the children involved in the study had been randomly assigned to receive the additional milk or not, but that the children's teachers were responsible for the randomisation and were able to reallocate the children. This led to a *selection bias* because the teachers could alter the group allocation. This 'juggling' of the randomisation probably went something like this . . . Harry was the next child to be randomised. His teacher threw the die, or looked up the next number in a random numbers table. The result was that Harry should go into the control group, so no extra milk. But the teacher thought about it. Harry was fairly short for his age and slightly underweight. The teacher felt that Harry could really do with the extra milk. Then there was Jack. Jack was growing just fine – tall and maybe even a little overweight. The teacher thought he did not need the extra milk, so she put Jack in before Harry, so Jack was allocated to the no extra milk group. Harry then got the next allocation in the list, which just happened to be to the extra milk group. The result was that the teachers ended up allocating more lighter and shorter children to the intervention group. Consequently, that by the end of the study all that had happened was the shorter, lighter children in the intervention group were only starting to catch up with their taller, heavier peers in the control group. If it had not been for this bias, the conclusion of the research may well have been that extra milk did have an effect on increasing height and weight.

There is a procedure to avoid this type of *allocation bias*. Someone completely independent of the care of the children could have allocated them (using the random numbers) to the intervention or control groups. This would have made it much harder for anyone involved in the children's care to have swapped children between groups. A well-conducted RCT should take steps to prevent any alteration to the sequence of randomisation, and such steps should be recorded in the write-up of the study.

Systematic reviews

When the results of several existing research reports or papers are collated, this is known as *secondary research*. *Systematic reviews* are a form of secondary research whose particular features mean that they come at the top of the 'levels of evidence' outlined in Figure 3.1.

A systematic review can be defined as:

A review of all the literature on a particular topic, which has been systematically identified, appraised and amalgamated to give a summary answer.

They are normally based on a synthesis of findings from relevant RCTs, and are seen as the very best source of research to support decision making about questions of effectiveness. This is because the conclusions they draw are based on a 'summing-up' of an exhaustive search of all the high quality research on a particular question or topic.

Systematic reviews are *not the same* as narrative reviews. When researchers step onto the lengthy path of undertaking a systematic review, they sign up to find *all* the relevant research in a particular field and to being completely transparent about how their search was conducted (for example, which databases they searched and what time period was covered). They also *critically appraise* the research they gather based on pre-defined criteria, only including in the review the findings from papers that meet these criteria. This approach prevents authors writing about the effectiveness of, for example, intermediate care, based on the ten articles they happen to have to hand, or in their filing cabinet. Equally, the design of systematic reviews avoids, for example, arguing for the effectiveness of cognitive-behavioural therapy for young people with behavioural problems by reference to only those papers supporting this idea, and ignoring any papers that contradict it. (You could get away with either of these in a narrative review.)

Systematic reviews sometimes include a *meta-analysis*. This involves pooling the results from studies exploring similar interventions to give a single estimate of effectiveness. More weight is normally given to results from larger studies.

This sounds like something technical, and it is. However, knowing the ins and outs of how a meta-analysis is conducted is far less relevant to the evidence-based practitioner than knowing the type of useable information it can give to aid decision making. Consequently, if a practice decision is based on the findings of a meta-analysis, it is grounded in the combined results of several pieces of research.

Systematic reviews using a meta-analysis are particularly useful if some RCTs suggest an intervention is effective and others suggest it is not. For example, imagine that Figure 3.9 below shows the results from six well-conducted RCTs which have each looked at the effectiveness of residential rehabilitation as compared to usual services in terms of increasing the independence of older people.

Where a black square falls to the left of the dark vertical line, the study showed that the intervention was more effective than usual services. Where a black square falls to the right of the dark vertical line, the study showed that usual care was more effective than residential rehabilitation. Where the square lands directly on the line, this shows no difference in the resulting independence of the older people who received the intervention and those who did not. If Mrs Patel's social worker were to consider the results of these studies individually the information would be very unhelpful, as some suggest that residential rehabilitation is likely to be effective for Mrs Patel, and others

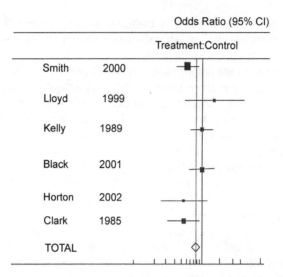

Figure 3.9   Systematic review – increasing the independence of older people

that it is not. However, when the study results are synthesised the message becomes clearer. It *does* appear that residential rehabilitation works better than usual care in increasing the independence of older people because the diamond, or summary statistic, at the bottom of this diagram, which reflects the combined data from all six studies, falls on the treatment side of the dark vertical line.

Some potential sources of bias in a systematic review

Although systematic reviews are seen as being at the top of the levels of evidence, they are not immune to bias. Bias may derive from a poor search strategy, for example, using just one or two databases to locate relevant studies, or failing to hand-search. This may result in only a proportion of the relevant studies being identified and conclusions being drawn on the basis of a subgroup of papers. Systematic reviews should be thorough in identifying relevant studies and the search process documented so that it could be reproduced by others.

Bias may also derive from the inclusion/exclusion criteria drawn up for the review. For example, limiting the investigation to research published only in English, or to a certain time period, may mean that the effectiveness of a particular approach is under or overestimated because a sub-sample of literature has not been considered. If restrictions are placed on the papers searched for, they should be justified by the authors of a review. In addition, bias may arise if only one person searches or screens studies for inclusion or assesses the quality of papers since judgments made could be prone to personal bias and mistakes. Systematic reviews are usually conducted by a team of researchers, so that the selection or rejection of studies and the extraction of data from accepted research can be double checked.

A final point to make here is that systematic reviews are limited by the availability of the primary research that their compilers have to draw on in relation to the review question. In areas where there are insufficient primary studies of good quality – and many areas of social care practice have been insufficiently investigated using experimental models – systematic reviews cannot be completed.

Bearing in mind these factors, if there was a systematic review of the effectiveness of residential rehabilitation units for older people, or the effectiveness of cognitive-behavioural therapy for children with behavioural problems, the social workers in our scenarios would do well to draw on their findings in helping Mrs Patel and Joshua.

Why different 'levels' in quantitative research design?

The levels described in Figure 3.1 do not detail all the types of quantitative research design that exist. That is not the intention of this chapter. The aim is to give a flavour of the main types of design that social care practitioners are likely to encounter, and to illustrate why research higher up the levels tend to give more trustworthy answers. The need to have answers that you can be more confident of is obvious, but (we think) always worth reiterating. Critical appraisal has no point unless it is connected back to the service user, to practice, or to policy decisions. If decision making based on quantitative research relies on evidence from lower in the illustrated levels, decisions made may not lead to better care for service users.

Having this framework of levels can also help busy social workers decide what to take the time and trouble to read, and what to ignore. A quick search on the electronic databases CareData or ASSIA (see Chapters 2 and 7) demonstrates that a wealth of research studies and reports have been conducted on all types of issues relevant to social care. Such a mass of information can leave practitioners wondering what is worth finding or obtaining, let alone reading. A rule of thumb, especially when looking for studies on the effectiveness of interventions, is to start by searching for a systematic review. If there is one that answers the question to be asked, which has been conducted in a manner as free of bias as possible, this should be turned to first. If no systematic review exists, look to see if there are any RCTs that answer the question. If not, are there quasi-experimental studies?

ɔrk of levels gives a guide for sifting through the pile of research
s may face, enabling them to sort the wheat from the chaff.

Qu. tative research: finding out about meanings, experiences, views and events

Hopefully, the practitioners working with Mrs Patel and Joshua will have used the levels of evidence outlined in Figure 3.1 as a guide for considering the effectiveness of a stay in a residential rehabilitation unit and a multi-disciplinary programme based on cognitive-behavioural principles. However, quantitative research will *not* tell the social workers how these interventions are likely to be experienced by Mrs Patel or Joshua. This sort of information can be drawn from qualitative research.

Qualitative research involves:

. . . the development of concepts which help us to understand social phenomena in natural (rather than experimental) settings, giving due emphasis to the meanings, experiences, and views of all the participants [9].

Qualitative inquiry can help us understand a particular situation or circumstance, allowing for explanation and interpretation. It can be used to examine a phenomenon that has not been previously investigated, and is especially useful for exploring sensitive or complex issues. Qualitative research can investigate the attitudes of service users and carers, giving a deeper insight into the ramifications of an intervention by recording people's experiences of receiving professional care. This can help in changing and improving services.

Types of questions that qualitative research might answer include:

- What are social workers' views of the use of standardised measures in their work?
- Why do some people with physical disabilities appear to gain little benefit from supported housing?
- How do teenage mothers cope with looking after their infant?

As we have argued, quantitative and qualitative research are complementary. Quantitative research can tell us about the probable effectiveness of services for Mrs Patel and Joshua; qualitative research can give us an insight into what their experiences of the interventions are likely to be. Most importantly, qualitative approaches can help us understand what is more and less important to people. It is, as many service users have discovered to their cost, all too easy to be very effective at doing the wrong thing.

Different methods, not different levels

The forms of qualitative research design that social workers are most likely to encounter were shown in Figure 3.1. These are displayed not as a series of levels, but as a set of methods, each of which is described below.

Interviews

Qualitative interviews can be *semi-structured* or *unstructured*. For semi-structured interviews, researchers draw up, in advance, a series of topics and/or questions that they wish to ask. They will sequence these to fit the flow of the conversation, changing the wording and order to suit what is being said, concentrating on some topics more than others, depending on interviewees' responses. Hence, the researcher follows areas of interest brought up by the participant, whilst keeping clearly in mind the research question.

Unstructured interviews are less pre-shaped. Researchers may have a broad topic that they wish to discuss, but will not generate questions in advance. For example, they might wish to investigate the views of parents about a multi-disciplinary, cognitive-behavioural programme for their children. The interviewer may start by asking; 'What do you think of the programme?', and then ask additional questions to ensure that the interview flows and provides data relevant to the research topic. However, they will not have prepared these questions in advance.

Interviews are an appropriate method when a researcher wants to generate very detailed information and obtain an in-depth view of individual experiences. A qualitative interview should enable an interviewee to think through their views, opinions and answers, and express them in their own terms or words.

For example, Mrs Patel's social worker could draw on a qualitative study called the *User Voice* [10] to gain an insight into how it might be for Mrs Patel to stay in a rehabilitation unit. The aim of this research was to determine what older people felt worked and what could have worked better whilst staying in such a unit. One-to-one semi-structured interviews were conducted with older people approximately a year after their stay.

However, Mrs Patel's social worker needs to check the study for sources of bias. This might be introduced in the following ways:

- *The location of the interviews.* Older people may feel more comfortable being interviewed at home, on their 'own ground', rather than in a social services office or a GP clinic. Where an interview takes place might therefore influence the detail of participants' responses.
- *Who conducted the interviews.* A research interview is not an ordinary conversation and requires facilitation by a skilled research interviewer. Also,

the answers interviewees give may depend on who interviews them. To go back to the study involving older people who had spent some time in a rehabilitation unit, if these participants were interviewed by an occupational therapist on the rehabilitation team, they might have been guarded or painted the intervention in an overly positive light for fear of future services being affected. Ideally, the interviewer should be *independent* of the service or intervention being evaluated.

- *Who was present when the interviews were conducted.* Research interviews are ordinarily one-to-one, that is, one interviewer, one interviewee. However, sometimes another person sits in. For example, an elderly woman may wish to be interviewed with her husband present. Having someone else there is likely to alter the dynamics of an interview and the answers given. For example, in the *User Voice* study the researcher might have asked what participants felt was the greatest benefit of going to the rehabilitation unit. An interviewee might have wished to say that he really had no choice because his wife was not able to manage with him at home at the time. He might be less inclined to disclose this information with his wife present.
- *The length of the interviews.* Different length interviews will give different depths of perspective and impressions of the issue being investigated. It is likely that richer, more detailed information will be provided during a two hour compared to a ten minute interview.

When reading a study based on qualitative interviews, these issues need to be kept in mind. Similar considerations also apply to focus group studies, to which we now turn.

Focus groups

A focus group is a meeting to discuss a particular subject, to hear people's views about a specific issue, or to discuss experiences of a service or certain situation. For example, a focus group could be held with parents of children with behavioural problems to find out what they felt the benefits had been of a multi-disciplinary, cognitive-behavioural programme for their children. (This could be a piece of research that Joshua's social worker might wish to draw on.) Focus groups tend to have between four and 10 participants. Their value is their interactive element – people consider their views together. This provides an excellent forum for attitudes, opinions and seeds of ideas to form and develop. While focus groups are not representative in the usual sense, if properly constructed, they will contain participants whose views cover the most important variations of opinion in the topic under discussion. The key feature of a focus group is that while the facilitators may determine the general topic, the issues and perspectives discussed, and their relative importance, are determined by the participants.

However, before Joshua's social worker uses the findings of a focus group study to inform her decision making about Joshua and his family, she needs to consider the possible sources of bias that may be introduced in focus groups. Focus groups can be difficult to facilitate and need to be run by researchers with previous experience. Biased information may be produced if discussion dries up, so little data are produced; the facilitator does not keep participants to the topic, so extraneous details are collected; or if one or two people dominate, so their views are over-represented in the information collected, with the opinions of the majority under-represented. An experienced researcher should work to stop these problems from occurring.

Observational studies

This approach involves a researcher (or team of researchers) entering a situation and directly seeing what happens.

Observation may be *covert*, whereby those being observed do not know this is the case. For example, a researcher might enter a mental health day centre pretending to be a service user, if the question they are addressing is 'what benefits do people with mental health problems gain from attending a day centre?' The advantage of covert observational studies is that they enable actions to be viewed in a natural setting, without changes in behaviour occurring because people know they are being watched. However, this approach is extremely questionable ethically, and is more likely to be a feature of journalism rather than social care research.

In *overt* observational studies, the researcher is explicit about their interest in the situation and setting, and gains informed consent from the study participants.

The researcher might act as a *participant observer* or a *non-participant observer*. Participant observation means the researcher engages in the activities of those being observed. For example, if the research question was 'how do mothers and fathers differ in parenting classes?', the participant observer would carry out the tasks set for those attending parenting classes. Non-participant observation means the researcher remains detached from the situation; they might watch social workers talking to an 'at risk' family, if the research question was 'how do social workers interact with parents of 'at risk' children?'

Observational studies are a valuable way of determining how systems operate or how people behave in given situations. They are the only method for gleaning this type of information which is not filtered through the perceptions of people who are part of that system. For example, if Mrs Patel's social worker wanted some details of how staff in rehabilitation units work towards *enabling* service users, rather than doing tasks for them, qualitative research that has conducted interviews with unit staff could be informative. However, this would only give details about the ideology of the unit and what the staff *aim* to do; it may not reflect how it *actually* happens. This could be assessed in an observational study.

Observational studies, like all research designs, are prone to bias. Potential sources of bias in such research include:

- *Watching it can alter it.* If study participants know they are being observed and details are being recorded of what they are doing or saying, this is likely to affect their behaviour. This 'researcher effect' can be kept to a minimum. For example, if different people are observed on a number of occasions the observation will be less likely to influence their behaviour.

- *Being part of it can alter it.* To help participants overcome the feeling of 'being watched' the researcher might participate in the situation. However, the very presence of the researcher may alter the nature of the interactions between people. The role of the evidence-based practitioner is to weigh up how much effect this might have on the study findings.

General issues to look out for in qualitative research

For all forms of qualitative research there are a number of general principles which can influence the trustworthiness of study findings.

How the research was conducted

The *sampling* approach used can affect a study's conclusions. As the goal of qualitative research is to further understanding of a situation or phenomenon, researchers will look for *breadth of opinion* and, therefore, will aim to involve all key individuals. For example, if Joshua's social worker found an interview-based study that explored what children themselves thought of the programme they had received, this might include boys and girls of all ages, with a broad range of behaviour problems. The parameters of the research sample should always be made clear, that is, who is and is not included, so that the reader can determine for whom the results are, and are not, likely to apply.

How the data were recorded

If *only* notes are taken during the course of an interview this may bias the conclusions drawn. It is very difficult to conduct a semi-structured or unstructured interview well and take notes at the same time. The interview may be rendered disjointed, breaking any rapport and making the interviewee less inclined to disclose details. Or, in an effort to maintain continuity, the interviewer may make few, patchy notes and try to recall what was said when the interview has finished. Neither is satisfactory. This bias can be overcome if consent is obtained to tape-record interviews, enabling the researcher to give full attention to the interviewee whilst also getting a verbatim account of what was said. Tape-recording is possibly even more important when conducting focus groups. Effectively facilitating a focus group, whilst note taking, is almost impossible. Tape-recordings of focus groups or interviews should be transcribed verbatim. The temptation is to summarise what was said. This is problematic as the researcher will start to impose their own biases about what they think is important and all the data collected will not be systematically analysed.

With observational studies it is more difficult to judge whether findings have been biased by the researcher's background or viewpoint. This is because, ordinarily, they will only make notes about the situation they are actually observing. Use of video-recording may minimise biases, but this is not often employed because of its logistical complications and potential intrusiveness. If the only method of data collection is the use of written notes, it is especially important that the researcher provides a clear description of their background and viewpoint, and reflects on how this may have affected the study and results. For example, an older person as researcher, who has used rehabilitation services, is likely to come to different conclusions to those of an occupational therapist who provides the service, or of an independent researcher.

How the data were analysed

A method of *analysis* is essential in all qualitative research. Recording random recollections of a few people who stayed in a rehabilitation unit is *not* qualitative research, although, unfortunately, it is often mislabelled as such. Qualitative research is underpinned by a *process* of analysis, which means the reader can clearly see *how* the conclusions have been drawn.

Analysis in qualitative research often involves breaking down data, such as interview or focus group transcripts, and *coding* this information. Transcripts are read and labelled according to what different parts or sections are about. These codes are then grouped or clustered into *themes*, which are recurring patterns or ideas. Initial themes are collapsed into overarching ones that summarise the main ideas emerging from the data. There are various methods or techniques for analysing qualitative data, such as grounded theory and discourse analysis.

A clear approach to analysis should prevent the qualitative researcher from drawing their favoured conclusions and 'cherry picking' quotes to fit. The research report should be clear that all relevant viewpoints have been incorporated and enough original data given to enable the reader to get a feel for what was said or done by those involved in the research (although word limits for journal articles mean this is often hard to achieve). Contradictory examples to the main conclusions should also be given to highlight that all data have been considered and systematically examined.

Qualitative research is an iterative process. For instance, five interviews might be conducted with children who have had a multi-disciplinary programme for their behaviour problems, the aim of the interviews being to explore their views of the programme. The transcripts of the interviews are analysed and show that the children have raised a number of issues. The researcher will continue interviewing because there are more themes or ideas likely to still be raised. Analysis of the transcripts of another five interviews shows that the themes are starting to repeat. After another five interviews *no new themes are emerging from the data*. This is labelled as the point of *data saturation*. Sample size in qualitative research is usually determined by this point. Well-conducted qualitative research will continue until data saturation is reached.

In analysing qualitative data, there are additional techniques that can be used to minimise bias and increase the trustworthiness of findings:

- *Triangulation*. This involves using multiple sources of information or data collection procedures. For example, data can be triangulated with other existing research, or both qualitative and quantitative methods can be used to address an issue, or data might be gathered in different ways (for example, through focus groups, interviews or observations).
- *Inter-rater reliability*. One researcher may check the themes produced by another to see how far they agree that they are grounded in the data. This second person will act as, 'a "devil's advocate" . . . alerting researchers to . . . potentially competing explanations' [11].
- *Respondent validation*. Preliminary findings are shown to study participants and they are asked whether this represents what was said. The aim of this process is to ensure participants' thoughts or actions are faithfully reported.

Narrative data are now commonly managed using computer packages, such as NUDIST or Atlas Ti. These organise and order data, but *do not* analyse it.

Bias revisited

Completely eliminating bias in a research study is not possible. However, potential biases can be *minimised*. Evidence-based practitioners must explore whether steps have been taken within a project to keep bias to a minimum. Where this is not possible, they have to weigh up the extent to which biases may have affected the overall study findings. The bottom line is: 'Is this piece of research trustworthy enough for me to use it to inform my practice?'

Relevance

We hope by now you are convinced of the need to have not just any 'evidence-base', or pile of research papers, but one which is made up of information that is trustworthy and rigorous. However, there is little point in having *rigour* without *relevance*. For example, an RCT might be well conducted in a way that means it is free from bias and gives trustworthy findings, but its conclusion is that the conduct of children with behaviour problems improves significantly if they are visited five days a week for eight weeks by a specially trained social worker (as compared to children who do not get the visits). Good news no doubt, but what social worker has the time to visit a child every working day for two months, and where can the social worker get the necessary specialist training? This research is unlikely to be relevant to the practitioner working with Joshua.

The relevance of a research study can be judged by asking: 'How useful are the findings to me, my clients, my work, or my organisation?' This can be broken down into more specific questions. We will come back to Mrs Patel to illustrate this.

Mrs Patel's social worker finds a piece of qualitative research that has looked at older people's experiences of staying in a residential rehabilitation unit. In judging the relevance of this research, the following questions are considered:

- *Do the study participants differ from Mrs Patel in ways which might give different results?* For example, are they in their 60s, whereas Mrs Patel is 82? Have they had a stroke, whilst Mrs Patel fractured the neck of her femur? Were they living at home alone, whereas Mrs Patel lives with her husband? Are there significant cultural differences? Are any of these differences likely to have an effect on the study's relevance to my client?
- *Does my local setting differ much from the setting in the research?* Is the setting urban, whilst I work in a rural community? Are the service users leaving acute hospital, whilst Mrs Patel is currently in a community hospital?
- *Can I provide the same service or intervention in my setting?* Is this type of service available to me locally? If not, is there funding, facilities, staff time available to provide it? Do staff in my department have the specific skills and training to deliver it?

Trustworthiness is vital in research, but if a study is not relevant to your service users, there is little point taking the time and effort to read and critically appraise it in its entirety.

Critical appraisal: not just an optional add-on

The evidence-based practitioner never looks at a research study or report without first putting on their critical reading glasses. Critical appraisal may sound like a complex undertaking, but the more you do it the easier it becomes. Understanding all the jargon or terminology found in research papers is not necessary; what is essential is taking a critical approach by considering the trustworthiness and relevance of the research.

Conclusion

Having critically appraised a piece of research, you may arrive at one of two conclusions:

- You may not feel happy about a study's trustworthiness and, therefore, do not use it to inform your practice decisions.
- The research appears trustworthy and you feel comfortable using it to help make decisions about the care of service users.

Only by critically appraising and thinking about the relevance of a piece of research can you be confident about applying this information to assist with your decision making, thus ensuring that you are doing the best for those who rely on you for help.

And finally . . . you don't have to do it all on your own

The Centre for Evidence-Based Social Services has devised a number of 'tools' to guide evidence-based practitioners in working through different forms of research papers or reports. These draw heavily on the work of the Critical Appraisal Skills Programme (CASP) [12] and emphasise what to look for to assess bias and to obtain a picture of the trustworthiness of a piece of research. We complete this chapter by providing these tools as examples of how the process of critical appraisal can be structured. These are critical thinking tools for:

- randomised controlled trials
- quasi-experimental trials
- qualitative studies

Each tool begins with two screening questions, which are designed to help determine whether it is worth taking the time, trouble and effort to read the whole report. If you find the answer to these first two questions to be 'no', it is very unlikely that the research study is trustworthy, or it is not possible to tell whether it is trustworthy or not due to it being poorly written. (The biggest problem in the write-up of social care research is inadequate details given in the methods sections.) If this is the case, there may seem little point reading the report in detail. By following the sequence of questions in the tools relevant to the kind of study you wish to appraise, you will be able to reach an informed judgement as to how much trust you can place in the findings of a particular study.

Centre for Evidence-Based Social Services Critical Thinking Tool

1. Randomised Controlled Trials (RCTs)

This critical thinking tool is designed to help you work through and make sense of research articles that report the results of randomised controlled trials (RCTs). This tool is a complement to our 'Critical Thinking for Social Care Staff' training courses, which will give you the background knowledge to help you use this tool.

The 13 questions that follow are designed to help you:
• Appraise the quality of the research.
• Decide whether you feel the study is trustworthy enough to justify using its results to inform your practice.
• Consider how relevant the research is to your own service(s).

The main questions are in bold. These are followed by points to consider to help think through your answers.

The first two questions are for 'screening' purposes. If you answer 'yes' to both of these it is worth working through the rest of the paper. However, if you answer 'no' to either of them the trustworthiness of the study is questionable. This means you would not want to apply its findings to your practice, or use them in your client decision making. Therefore, it is probably not worth taking the time, trouble and effort to read the rest of the paper in detail.

If you find that you answer 'yes' to most of the 13 questions, the quality of the study is likely to be high and worthwhile using in practice decision making. If you answer 'no' to the majority of the questions, the opposite is true.

The questions are adapted from Guyatt GH, Sackett DL, and Cook DJ, Users' guides to the medical literature. II. How to use an article about therapy or prevention. *JAMA* 1993; 270 (21): 2598–2601 and *JAMA* 1994; 271(1): 59–63

This tool draws heavily from the tools developed by the 'Critical Appraisal Skills Programme', Milton Keynes Primary Care Trust 2002.

Please circle the appropriate answers to the questions below:

Screening
1. Were the aims of the research clear?
                                                Y   N

Who was the *client group* being investigated?
What was the *intervention* being given?
What services/intervention did the *control* group receive?
What *outcomes* were considered?

Please write in the box what the aims of the research were, or what the research question was. (Everything that is done in the piece of research should relate to this question.)

```
┌─────────────────────────────────────────────────────────────┐
│                                                             │
│                                                             │
│                                                             │
│                                                             │
│                                                             │
└─────────────────────────────────────────────────────────────┘
```

2. Was a randomised controlled trial the right sort of research design to use to answer the research question?
                                                Y   N

Did the study aim to find out about the effectiveness of an intervention or service?
Is it worth continuing?   Y   N

Methods
3. Were the participants allocated to the intervention or control groups in a way that really was *random*?
                                    Y   Not enough   N
                                            detail given

For example, were random number tables, the roll of a die, the flip of a coin, names out of a hat used, rather than allocating people alphabetically or consecutively?

4. Was allocation in the study *concealed*?
                                    Y   Not enough   N
                                            detail given

Was the process of allocation done as *independently* as possible from all those involved in the care of people taking part in the study, e.g. making sure it was not a social worker providing the clients' care who allocated clients to the intervention or control groups?
Were steps taken to stop people 'tinkering' with which groups people were allocated to, e.g. by using sealed envelopes?

5. **If it was possible to do so, were the participants, the people providing the intervention/service, and the assessors 'blind' to, or unaware of, group allocation?**

    Y   To some   N
          extent

    'Blinding' is not always possible.

    Having 'blind' *assessors* is the most important element of 'blinding'.

6. **Were the intervention and control group well *matched* at the beginning of the study?**

    Y   To some   N
          extent

    For example, did the researchers produce a table listing key demographic information (e.g. age, sex) separately for the intervention and control groups?

    Were there any key differences between the groups at baseline, which might, in part, account for any differences in outcome (known as *confounders*)?

7. **Was the number of participants in the study justified?**

    Y   Not enough   N
          detail given

    Is there a *power calculation* which showed that there were enough people in the study to find a difference in outcome between the intervention and control groups if one existed? (If there were not enough participants, the study may not have found a difference purely because too few people took part.)

8. **Were the participants in the intervention and control groups followed up, and data collected, in the same way?**

    Y   To some   N
          extent

    Did the two groups complete the same measures, at the same time points, in the same way?

Results

9. **Were *all* the participants who started off in the study accounted for at the end?**

    Y   N

    Did the researchers make clear what had happened to *all* the participants at the end of the study? (Even if they were no longer taking part they should be accounted for.)

    Were *all* the participants followed up? If not, what degree of 'loss to follow-up' was there?

Were the people who 'dropped out' different in any significant way from the people who remained in the study?

Were all participants' outcomes analysed by the groups to which they were originally allocated – *intention-to-treat analysis*. (If this is not done the whole point of the randomisation breaks down.)

10. Are the results clearly presented and are they appropriate?

Y   To some   N

extent

Do the results answer the *research question*?

Do the results answer the research question without going off at tangents – *data trawling or fishing*. (One in 20 results will be statistically significant by chance alone.)

Do the statistics seem appropriate?

Were the statistical tests used the correct sorts of tests to use?

Briefly describe the main results:

Conclusions

11. Are the conclusions drawn supported by the study results?

Y   To some   N

extent

Is what is said in the conclusion/discussion section justified by what the results actually show?

Ethics

12. Were ethical issues addressed?

Y   To some   N

extent

Did the researchers seek approval for the research from an ethics committee?

Was it clear how the study was explained to the participants?

Did the researchers obtain informed consent from participants?

Was confidentiality ensured?

Relevance

13. Is this study relevant to your clients and/or practice?

Y   To some   N
       extent

Were the participants in the study similar to your clients? (Is there any reason to think that conducting the RCT with your clients would have given different results?)

Would people in your client group have been excluded from the study (on the basis of its inclusion and exclusion criteria)? If so, this might make you question the relevance of the research to your practice.

Is your local setting similar to that in the study?

Would it be possible for you to provide the same intervention/service in your setting?

Centre for Evidence-Based Social Services Critical Thinking Tool

2. Quasi-experimental studies

This critical thinking tool is designed to help you work through and make sense of research articles that report the results of quasi-experimental studies. This tool is a complement to our 'Critical Thinking for Social Care Staff' training courses, which will give you the background knowledge to help you use this tool.

The 13 questions that follow are designed to help you:

• Appraise the quality of the research.

• Decide whether you feel the study is trustworthy enough to justify using its results to inform your practice.

• Consider how relevant the research is to your own service(s).

The main questions are in bold. These are followed by points to consider to help think through your answers.

The first two questions are for 'screening' purposes. If you answer 'yes' to both of these it is worth working through the rest of the paper. However, if you answer 'no' to either of them the trustworthiness of the study is questionable. This means you would not want to apply its findings to your practice, or use them in your client decision making. Therefore, it is probably not worth taking the time, trouble and effort to read the rest of the paper in detail.

If you find that you answer 'yes' to most of the 13 questions, the quality of the study is likely to be high and worthwhile using in practice decision making. If you answer 'no' to the majority of the questions, the opposite is true.

The questions are adapted from Guyatt GH, Sackett DL, and Cook DJ, Users' guides to the medical literature. II. How to use an article about therapy or prevention. *JAMA* 1993; 270 (21): 2598–2601 and *JAMA* 1994; 271(1): 59–63

This tool draws heavily from the tools developed by the 'Critical Appraisal Skills Programme', Milton Keynes Primary Care Trust 2002.

Please circle the appropriate response in the questions below

Screening

1. Were the aims of the research clear?

Y   N

Who was the *client group* being investigated?
What was the *intervention* being given?
What services/intervention did the *control* group receive?
What *outcomes* were considered?

Please write in the box what the aims of the research were, or what the research question was. (Everything that is done in the piece of research should relate to this question.)

```
┌─────────────────────────────────────────────────────────┐
│                                                         │
│                                                         │
│                                                         │
│                                                         │
│                                                         │
└─────────────────────────────────────────────────────────┘
```

2. Was a quasi-experimental study the right sort of research design to use to answer the question?

Y   N

Did the study aim to find out about the effectiveness of an intervention or service, but it would have been very complicated or impossible to have conducted a randomised controlled trial?
Is it worth continuing?

Y   N

Methods

3. Do the researchers justify why a randomised controlled trial would not have been possible or desirable?

Y   To some   N
                   extent

4. Were participants recruited to the intervention and control groups in a way that minimised bias and confounders?

Y   To some   N
                 extent

For example, were the same inclusion and exclusion criteria applied to both groups?

5. Were the intervention and control groups well *matched* at the beginning of the study?

Y   To some   N
                 extent

For example, did the researchers produce a table listing key demographic information (e.g. age, sex) separately for the intervention and control groups?

Were there any key differences between the groups at baseline, which might, in part, account for any differences in outcome (known as *confounders*)?

6. Was the number of participants in the study justified?

Y   Not enough   N
                 detail given

Is there a *power calculation* which showed that there were enough people in the study to find a difference in outcome between the intervention and control groups if one existed? (If there were not enough participants, the study may not have found a difference purely because too few people took part.)

7. Were the participants in the intervention and control groups followed up, and data collected, in the same way?

Y   To some   N
                 extent

Did the two groups complete the same measures, at the same time points, in the same way?

Results

8. Were *all* the participants who started off in the study accounted for at the end?

Y   N

Did the researchers make clear what had happened to *all* the participants at the end of the study? (Even if they were no longer taking part they should be accounted for).

Were *all* the participants followed-up? If not, what degree of 'loss to follow-up' was there?
Were the people who 'dropped out' different in any significant way from the people who remained in the study?

9. **Are the results clearly presented and are they appropriate?**

Y To some N
extent

Do the results answer the *research question?*
Do the results answer the research question without going off at tangents – *data trawling or fishing.* (One in 20 results will be statistically significant by chance alone.)
Do the statistics seem appropriate?
Were the statistical tests used the correct sorts of tests to use?

Briefly describe the main findings:

10. **Have the researchers taken account of potential confounding factors in the analysis?**

Y To some N
extent

For example was regression or covariate analysis used, adjusting for likely confounding factors?

Conclusions

11. **Are the conclusions drawn supported by the study results?**

Y To some N
extent

Is what is said in the conclusion/discussion section justified by what the results actually show?

Ethics

12. **Were ethical issues addressed?**

Y To some N
extent

Did the researchers seek approval for the research from an ethics committee?

Was it clear how the study was explained to the participants?
Did the researchers obtain informed consent from participants?
Was confidentiality ensured?

Relevance

13. Is this study relevant to your clients and/or practice?

Y　　To some　　N
　　　 extent

Were the participants in the study similar to your clients? (Is there any reason to think that conducting the quasi-experimental study on your clients would have given different results?)
Would people in your client group have been excluded from the study (on the basis of its inclusion and exclusion criteria for participants)? If so, this might make you question the relevance of the research to your practice.
Is your local setting similar to that in the study?
Would it be possible for you to provide the same intervention/service in your setting?

Centre for Evidence-Based Social Services Critical Thinking Tool

3. Qualitative research

This critical thinking tool is designed to help you work through and make sense of qualitative research articles. This tool is a complement to our 'Critical Thinking for Social Care Staff' training courses, which will give you the background knowledge to help you use this tool.

The 13 questions that follow are designed to help you:
- Appraise the quality of the research.
- Decide whether you feel the study is trustworthy enough to justify using its results to inform your practice.
- Consider how relevant the research is to your own service(s).

The main questions are in bold. These are followed by points to consider to help think through your answers.

The first two questions are for 'screening' purposes. If you answer 'yes' to both of these it is worth working through the rest of the paper. However, if you answer 'no' to either of them the trustworthiness of the study is questionable. This means you would not want to apply its findings to your practice, or use them in your client decision making. Therefore, it is probably not worth taking the time, trouble and effort to read the rest of the paper in detail.

If you find that you answer 'yes' to most of the 13 questions, the quality of the study is likely to be high and worthwhile using in practice decision making. If you answer 'no' to the majority of the questions, the opposite is true.

This tool draws heavily from the tools developed by the 'national CASP collaboration for qualitative methodologies'. Milton Keynes Primary Care Trust 2002.

Please circle the appropriate answers to the questions below

Screening

1. Were the aims of the research clear?

Y   N

Was it clear why the researchers were carrying out the study?

Please write in the box what the aims of the research were, or what the research question was. (Everything that is done in the piece of research should relate to this question.)

```
┌─────────────────────────────────────────────────────┐
│                                                       │
│                                                       │
│                                                       │
│                                                       │
│                                                       │
│                                                       │
└─────────────────────────────────────────────────────┘
```

2. Was qualitative research the right sort of approach to use to answer the research question?

Y   N

Did the researchers aim to interpret or illuminate people's actions and/or their experiences?
Is it worth continuing?

Y   N

Methods

3. Was the research design used the most appropriate to address the aims of the study?

Y   N

For example, if interviews, focus groups or an observational design were used, was this appropriate?

4. Was the sampling strategy used for the study clear/appropriate?

Y   To some   N
extent

For example, did the researchers make clear how participants were selected to take part?
Was this appropriate in terms of answering the research question?
Were they clear about the parameters of their sample, i.e. those to be included and those to be excluded?

5. Was the number of participants in the study justified?

Y   To some   N
extent

For example, did the researchers state that data saturation had been reached?

6. Did the way that the data were collected fit with the aims of the study?

Y   To some   N
extent

Was it clear:
Where the data were collected? e.g. an office or people's own homes?
By *whom*? e.g. was this person an independent researcher, a service provider?
How the data were collected? e.g. using a focus group topic guide, unstructured interviews? Tape-recorded, videoed, hand written notes?
How *long* this took? e.g. were participants interviewed for 10 minutes or two hours? Were they observed once a week for two months, or just on one occasion?

7. Was data collection systematic?

Y   To some   N
extent

Did the researchers adopt a similar approach to collecting data with each participant involved in the study?
Was all the data recorded in the same way?

8. Was it clear how the data were analysed?

Y   To some   N
extent

For example, was it coded, themed?
What data analysis technique was used, e.g. grounded theory, discourse analysis, framework analysis?

Results

9. Are the results clearly presented/appropriate?

Y   To some   N
extent

Was it clear how the themes presented were derived?
Was there a sufficient amount of the original data presented to support how the data was interpreted?
Did the data that were presented support the study findings?
Did quotes come from a range of participants?
Did the researchers discuss data that did *not* support their findings?

Briefly describe the main results:

```
┌──────────────────────────────────────────────────────────┐
│                                                          │
│                                                          │
│                                                          │
│                                                          │
│                                                          │
└──────────────────────────────────────────────────────────┘
```

10. Were steps taken to increase the trustworthiness of the study findings?

Y   To some   N
extent

Did researchers feedback results to study participants and ask them to comment on their accuracy?
Did they triangulate their data in any way, e.g. with existing, relevant research, or via different research methods?
Did they ask a colleague to check their interpretation of the data?

11. Did the researchers critically examine their role, potential bias and influence on the study findings?

Y   To some   N
extent

For example, were their biases considered during data collection, analysis and selection of data for presentation?

Ethics

12. Were ethical issues addressed?

Y   To some   N
extent

Did the researchers seek approval for the research from an ethics committee?

Was it clear how the study was explained to participants?
Did the researchers obtain informed consent from participants?
Was confidentiality ensured?

Relevance

13. Is this study relevant to your clients and/or practice?

Y   To some   N
extent

Were the participants in the study similar to your clients? (Is there any reason to think that conducting the research with your clients would have given different results?)

Would people in your client group have been excluded from the study (on the basis of the sampling strategy)? If so, this might make you question the relevance of the research to your practice.

Is your local setting similar to that in the study?

Would it be possible for you to provide the same intervention/service in your setting?

References

[1] Crombie, I.K. (1996) *The Pocket Guide to Critical Appraisal: A Handbook for Health Care Professionals*. BMJ Publishing: London.

[2] Crombie, I.K. (1996) *The Pocket Guide to Critical Appraisal: A Handbook for Health Care Professionals*. BMJ Publishing: London p18.

[3] Lovering, K. and Caldwell, A. (2003) *Scallywags. Interagency Early Intervention Project for Children with Emotional and Behaviour Problems: Research Review and Project Evaluation*. Centre for Evidence-Based Social Services, University of Exeter.

[4] Trappes-Lomax, T., Ellis, A. and Fox, M. (2002) *Buying Time. An Evaluation and Cost Effectiveness Analysis of a Joint Health/Social Care Residential Rehabilitation Unit for Older People on Discharge From Hospital*. Centre for Evidence-Based Social Services, University of Exeter.

[5] Gambrill, E. (1997) *Social Work Practice: A Critical Thinker's Guide*. New York; Oxford: Oxford University Press.

[6] Greenhalgh, T. (2001) *How to Read a Paper: The Basics of Evidence Based Medicine*. 2nd edn, London: BMJ Publishing.

[7] 'Student' (1931) The Lanarkshire milk experiment. *Biometrika*: 23: 398–406.

[8] Altman, D.G. (1980) Statistics and ethics in medical research: collecting and screening data. *British Medical Journal*. 281: 1399–401.

[9] Pope, C. and Mays, N. (1996) Qualitative methods in health and health services research. In Mays, N. and Pope, C. (Eds.) *Qualitative Research in Health Care*. London: BMJ Publishing.

[10] Trappes-Lomax, T., Ellis, A., Terry, R. and Stead, J. (2003) *The User Voice I, II & III. Three Qualitative Studies of the Views of Older People Concerning Rehabilitation Services They Received in Hospital, in Social Services/NHS Residential Rehabilitation Units, and at Home*. Centre for Evidence-Based Social Services, University of Exeter.

[11] Barbour, R.S. (2001) Checklists for improving rigour in qualitative research: a case of the tail wagging the dog? *British Medical Journal*. 322: 1115–7.

[12] *www.phru.nhs.uk/casp/casp.htm*. Accessed 19.04.04.

Chapter 4

Understanding Statistics: A Gentle Guide to Numbers and What They Mean

The aims of this chapter are to:
- Provide a basic guide to making sense of the most common statistical terms and techniques.
- Illustrate these by use of practice examples.
- Help the reader to understand what statistics mean, without having to calculate them themselves.
- Outline some of the main points to look for when critically appraising results sections of quantitative research papers.

    Fear of harm ought to be proportional not merely to the gravity of the harm, but also to the probability of the event [1].

Statistics: what's the point?

Most social workers don't like statistics. A chill of apprehension settles over most of us on opening a textbook on statistics, even when (or especially when) the preface asserts that the treatise is aimed at the general reader, not the expert. Dislike, and even fear, of enumeration has a long pedigree. To the ancients, 'knowing one's number' was a divine prerogative. The second book of Samuel records the terrible vengeance wreaked by God when King David had the temerity to order a census of his army without prior celestial approval. Reducing humanity to the cold finality of a statistical table often engenders a similar uneasiness in members of a profession whose trade depends on making sense of complex and often competing narratives. Yet a basic grasp of what statistics mean is as necessary to social work as the capacity to listen, empathise and offer wise counsel. The inability to understand what numbers tell us, can lead to the exaggeration of small problems, whilst ignoring big ones.

All statistics reduce complex information to a numerical summary and, in doing so inevitably lose some of its complexity. However, in a world of competing welfare priorities, numbers matter. Public investment depends on how a social problem is perceived, with the two most important factors being how seriously, and how many, people are affected. The capacity to quantify a problem enables an issue to move from the domain of opinion, into the realm of fact.

Few social workers go through a working week without encountering a situation on which a statistical analysis could shed some light [2]. Is the size of a worker's caseload related to the amount of sick leave they take? How much do seasonal factors account for variation in the numbers of children on child protection registers? Will additional weekly home visits make it more likely that parents will attend sessions at family centres? Does sharing the content of a case file with service users increase user satisfaction? Is relationship counselling more successful when couples are seen alone or together? A basic grasp of some key statistical principles is sufficient for any practitioner to explore these questions, or to get someone else to do it for them. What is probably more important is having sufficient curiosity to want to try in the first place, and an appreciation that it is not the actual numbers that matter, but what the numbers mean.

What numbers mean

In the field of statistics, the numbers themselves are not really much use to the evidence-based practitioner – they are just labels. It is what we take the labels to represent, or what *the numbers mean* that is relevant. Only this way do statistics become useful in practice.

For example, you are told that the average depression score of young mothers coming to a family resource centre is 13. The number itself has no meaning. You are then told that 13 is on a scale that runs from 0 to 50, that 0 means no depression and 50 means the worst possible depression, and that the average depression score in the general population is 12. It is only then that the statistic starts to have some meaning or value to you as a practitioner.

You are given the statistics 'once in five years' and '30 times in five years'. In this form, the statistics tell you nothing of any value. It is only when they are related to the fact that these are the number of times that two of your clients, who are in their 90s, have been into hospital, that they have some meaning to you as a social care practitioner.

We start by describing what statistics are, and what the term statistics means.

What is/are statistics?

Statistics is an odd term because it has two (albeit connected) meanings:
• Statistics is the science of collecting and analysing numerical data.
• A *statistic* is a numerical fact or item.

So, *statistics* is about drawing together and examining information that has been recorded, or can be recorded, as numbers. Another way of saying this is that the information is quantifiable – numbers can be put to it. The number of times that a child changes foster carers, the number of times a social worker visits a client who is in residential care, the number of times someone with schizophrenia is admitted to an in-patient unit, are all examples of numerical or quantitative data. Likewise, a child's score on a measure of conduct disorder, an older person's independence score, a score of how well a multi-disciplinary team works together, are all forms of numerical or quantitative data.

All the pieces of numerical information described above are individual *statistics*. Statistics are often in the form of numbers (e.g. 35 of the 100 people on our client list live in supported housing), percentages (e.g. 35 per cent of our clients live in supported housing), or proportions (e.g. 0.35 of our clients live in supported housing). Statistics are also often expressed as averages.

How do most people think, feel, score, behave?: mean, median, mode

A social worker wants to find out the extent to which older people, who are in their 70s, 80s and 90s and living on their own, feel isolated. There is a reliable and valid questionnaire which measures self-perceived isolation and which has already been used throughout the country with other older people. This means that it is 'tried and tested', so you can be sure it does measure what it says it measures and that it will measure this in the same way time and time again. A representative sample of 250 older people (i.e. a group of older people who are similar to the wider population of older people in this age range) is recruited and a questionnaire sent to them. Two hundred replies are received (a good response rate). All the scores for each question are put onto a statistics computer package and the total self-perceived isolation score for each of the 200 people calculated. The social worker knows from the background information about the questionnaire that a total score of 0 is the worst possible sense of isolation a person can feel and a score of 100 means that someone does not feel isolated at all. What now? Well, a report could be written listing everyone's scores separately. However, this would make for a very long-winded document (e.g. the first person's isolation score was 20,

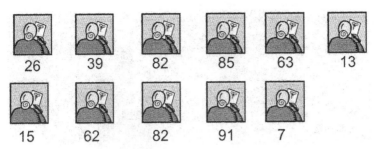

Figure 4.1   Calculating the mean – self-perceived social isolation

the second person's isolation score was 82, the third person's isolation score was 51 . . .), that no-one will read, and which will not really give an answer to the question set in the first place. What the social worker really wants to know is, on the whole, or *on average*, to what extent do older people in this age group feel isolated? This will help us decide whether there is a strong need to develop services or schemes that could help alleviate this sense of isolation, or whether, on the whole, the reports of older people themselves do not bear-out this perception of them feeling isolated.

There are three types of average that the social worker could use to report this *average* sense of isolation: *mean*, *median* and *mode*.

Mean

The mean is found by adding-up all the scores and dividing by the number of them. In this example, the social worker would add together all of the 200 total isolation scores and then divide by the number of them i.e. 200. Before sending out the questionnaires, the social worker decided to look separately at the average isolation scores of the people in their 90s. Eleven questionnaires were received from people in this age range. Their individual total scores are as shown in Figure 4.1.

To find the average isolation score of this subgroup, the social worker adds the 11 scores together, which gives a total of 565, and then divides by 11 (as there are 11 scores). This gives a *mean* self-perceived isolation score of 51.4. Therefore, the average self-perceived isolation score of this group of people in their 90s is about half-way between the greatest and the least feelings of isolation.

The mean is the type of average most commonly reported in results sections of quantitative research papers. However, it is not always appropriate to report the mean. This is the case if the data are *skewed*. 'Skewed' means that most of the data, or scores, cluster around a certain point, but that there is also a 'tail off' of scores. If, for example, the social worker found that in

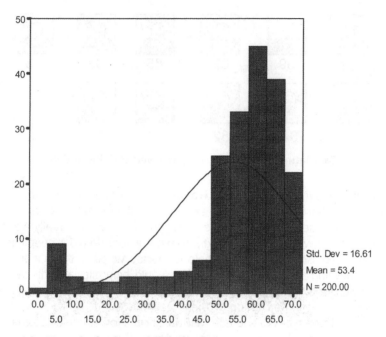

Figure 4.2   Negatively skewed distribution

the set of 200 questionnaires, most people scored between 50 and 70, but that quite a few had much lower scores, this would mean that the data were skewed, as illustrated in Figure 4.2.

A distribution that has a skew to the left – that is the tail is on the left side of the diagram – is known as negatively skewed, as the smallest values are displayed on the left. Equally, if nearly everyone scored between 20 and 40, but quite a few people also scored much higher, this would also be skewed data, as illustrated in Table 4.3.

In this figure, the *largest* values are on the left, and hence this is known as a positively skewed distribution. In both these Figures, you can see that the data have a peak and then a tail to one side. If the scores plot out like this, it shows that the data are skewed and it is not appropriate to report the mean.

There is little point reporting the mean when the data or scores are highly skewed because it does not really tell the reader how *most* people scored; the mean is distorted. You can see in Figure 4.2 that most people are scoring about 60. But, when all the scores are added together and divided by the number of them, the low scores distort this, and the mean comes out at about 53. Likewise, in Figure 4.3, you can see that most people are scoring about 30, but when all the scores are added together and divided by the

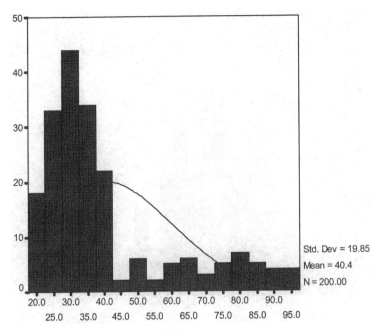

Figure 4.3   Positively skewed distribution

number of them, the high scores distort the mean, which comes out at about 40. It is only when the scores are in a symmetrical, bell-shape, or 'normal curve', that the mean gives a true picture of how *most* people score [3] as illustrated in Figure 4.4.

Median

The median always gives a true picture of the average score. This is because the actual values of the scores are not used when the median is worked out; only their order in the whole set of scores is taken into account. Consequently, a few really high or a few really low scores *cannot* distort the picture of what *most* people score.

This is how it works. The social worker would put all the 200 total scores in ascending order, starting with the low scores, through to the middling scores, and then up to the high scores. The median is the score that falls in the middle of the list. If we go back to the example of the 11 people in their 90s, the social worker would re-order the scores: 7, 13, 15, 26, 39, 62, 63, 82, 82, 85, 91. The score that falls in the middle of the list is 62, so this is the median. (If there is an even number of scores, the median is the mean of

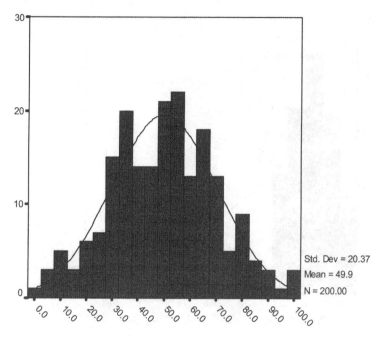

Figure 4.4   A normal distribution

the middle two. So, if there was an extra score in this set e.g. 6, 7, 13, 15, 26, 39, 62, 63, 82, 82, 85, 91, the median would be $39+62/2=50.5$).

Because it is always appropriate to give the median, you might ask why people bother with the mean at all. This is because the mean forms the basis of more advanced and more powerful statistical tests than the median does.

Mode

A third type of average you might come across is the mode, which is used far less than the mean or the median, but is useful for certain types of data. It is defined as 'the score that crops up most often', so is the one that occurs most frequently in any set of data. In the set of 11 scores of people in their 90s, the score 82 comes up twice, so this would be the mode. However, it is of little use in a small data set like this because it does not tell you what, on the whole, people scored.

Here are two examples where it is useful. A survey is conducted of a representative number of families in the UK to find out the average number of children per household. The survey results in a mean of 1.7 children per family. However, this is a bit of nonsense since you cannot have 0.7 of a child.

It would be more appropriate to use the 'number that crops up most often' here i.e. the mode. The average number of children in families in the UK using the mode is 2 – much more sensible.

When the social worker writes up, or reports on, the findings of the questionnaire survey examining the degree of isolation felt by older people, this will describe the characteristics of the people who returned the questionnaires. This is so that anyone reading the report can judge whether those that have been surveyed are like their own clients, otherwise they will not be able to tell whether the findings are relevant to them and their clients. The mean age of the group would be described, along with their mean independence levels and the mean length of time that they have lived alone. However, to describe their mean gender will make no sense. For example, if women were coded as '1' and men as '2', this might result in a mean gender of 1.3. It would be much more appropriate to describe the mode gender of the group: e.g. female.

Means, medians and modes can provide useful information about how *most* people feel, think, score, behave etc. However, these statistics become more useful if you are also told about the spread of the data. For example, knowing that the group of older people described above have a mean self-perceived isolation score of 51.4 tells you that their average sense of isolation is about half-way between feeling not isolated at all, to feeling totally isolated. However, it is likely that you would want to know whether pretty much everyone feels like this, or whether the scores are really quite spread out, suggesting that some people feel extremely isolated, while others do not feel isolated at all. This is where standard deviations and inter-quartile ranges come in.

How differently do people think, feel, score, behave?: standard deviation and inter-quartile ranges

Standard deviation

In the results sections of quantitative research papers, standard deviations are reported alongside mean scores and inter-quartile ranges are given with medians.

As autumn arrives, leaves will start to fall from the tree illustrated in Figure 4.5 [4]. The average, or mean, leaf will fall somewhere near the base of the tree – most of the leaves will fall here. Quite a few leaves will also fall a little distance away from the trunk. As you get further and further away from the tree, fewer and fewer leaves will fall here. The standard deviation would give you an idea of how far away from the tree most leaves are falling. Are they all mainly clustering around the mean leaf at the tree's base, or are they

Figure 4.5   Standard deviation (sd)

spreading out further and further away from the tree? Standard deviation is a measure of this spread or dispersion of leaves, scores, answers and so on.

Standard deviation can be thought of as the average (or mean) distance of all the scores from the mean, with a bit of mathematical adjustment to make it more useable in statistical tests. (If you are interested, see Bowers [5] for an excellent and clear account of how it is calculated.)

The way to get a handle of what a standard deviation in a research paper means is to think about it in relation to the size of the mean. The smaller the standard deviation (in relation to the mean) the more similar the scores; the larger the standard deviation (in relation to the mean) the more spread out the scores. In the example of the scores of the 11 people in their 90s, the mean score is 51.4 and the standard deviation is 32.2; the standard deviation is large in relation to the mean. This tells you that these 11 older people *do not* similarly rate their sense of isolation; there is quite a spread in their scores. As a rule of thumb, if the standard deviation is more than half the mean, the scores are really quite spread out, or skewed, and, as suggested, the authors should really give the median as the most appropriate type of average.

Inter-quartile range (IQR)

This is the alternative to reporting the standard deviation, when the median is given rather than the mean. As we have said, the median is the middle score when all the scores are put in ascending order. It is the score halfway up the list. The inter-quartile range is a measure of the distance between the score a quarter of the way up the list and the score three-quarters of the way up the list. In the example with the 11 older people, the scores would be re-ordered to: 7, 13, 15, 26, 39, 62, 63, 82, 82, 85, 91. The median is 62 because it is halfway up the list. The score a quarter of the way up the list is 15 and the score three-quarters of the way up the list is 82. Therefore, the IQR is 67 (82-15). This is large in relation to the median, which again shows that the scores of these 11 people are very spread.

Averages and measures of spread: what's the point?

There are two reasons why we have described types of average and measures of spread in some detail. Firstly, they are routinely used in results sections of quantitative research papers. If you do not have an understanding of what they are, or what they can tell you, you will be stumped at the first hurdle when critically appraising a results section of a research paper. Secondly, they are useful.

For example, imagine you have as a client a seven year old boy, who has been displaying behaviour problems for seven months. Both his parents are affected by schizophrenia; his mother has had the diagnosis for the last 10 years, and his father was diagnosed five years ago. You find a research report which has found positive effects from a social support programme for children who have parents with severe mental health problems and wonder if this might help your client. To be able to decide whether the results from the report are likely to apply to your client, you need to know what the clients who took part in the research were like. Fortunately, the report has a clear description of the children who took part:

The mean (sd) age of the children was 8 (2) years, and they had been displaying behaviour problems for a mean (sd) of 6 (2) months. The most common (modal) mental illness diagnosis of their parents was schizophrenia, who had had this mental health problem for a median (IQR) of 11 (7) years.

This descriptive information means you can make a judgment as to whether the findings of the research are applicable to your client. For example, you might consider whether or not the mean (standard deviation) age of 8 (2) of the children is relevant to your clients who are mainly in their early teens.

Performance Indicators, what they can and can't tell us

We hope by now that you are with us in our thinking that statistics is not about arbitrary facts and figures. The value of statistics lies in what the numbers reported mean.

Performance Indicators (PIs) are useful for social care staff in that they set estimated benchmark performance targets, and departments and authorities can assess how far they have travelled in achieving these targets. However, the interpretation of what achieving these targets, or getting a certain way towards meeting them *means* can be complex.

For example, let us take the Reimbursement Policy introduced the Department of Health [6]. This stipulates that all older people should be discharged from acute hospital within a certain number of days of it being decided that they are medically fit for discharge. Although many local authorities have taken advantage of pump priming finance to develop services to prevent delayed discharge, in essence the policy means that a social services department will have to reimburse the NHS for the extra days that a person remains in hospital if they are deemed to be responsible for holding up discharges. (We will put aside issues about the impact of this on partnership working, the cost of the administration needed to put this new policy in place and sort out the reimbursement charging and paying, and remain focused on statistics.) The department could put a PI in place to indicate the percentage of older people that they managed to get out of hospital within the time period stipulated. After six months of the Reimbursement Policy, the percentage might be found to be 70 per cent. A Director may think this is not quite good enough, so staff work on it for another six months. At the end of this period the figure has gone up – now 90 per cent of older people leave hospital within the period stipulated.

This looks good, but what does it mean? It could be that the social workers are working faster and are getting older people out of hospital more quickly. Or, it could be that in the preceding six months the clients seen had less complex needs, so a speedier hospital discharge was more straightforward anyway (summer compared to winter?). But, this PI does not tell us other, perhaps crucial, information. For example, what proportion of the discharges in the two six-month periods was appropriate or 'safe'? Were the social workers under such pressure to 'get people out' that they felt unable to do the full, thorough assessments that they would normally undertake? What percentage of people went home to a situation that was not really appropriate, or where there had not been sufficient time to put in place necessary services or aids and adaptations? How many of these older people who had quick discharges were back in hospital within the next couple of months because they were not really ready to go home in the first place? We have many examples of these unintended consequences at work in our field.

Performance Indicators can act as a useful audit tool; they can provide us with statistics that indicate to what extent targets are being achieved, and if the situation is unsatisfactory, how far we have to go to reach them. But, PIs alone cannot tell us which services are effective, or which interventions work.

Is it just fluke?: statistical tests

Social workers need to know, and be able to demonstrate, whether:
1. Things have improved (or not) for their clients.
2. If they have improved, whether this is due (or attributable) to a particular intervention or service.
3. Any improvement is a *real* improvement, or whether it is just due to chance.

For example, the social worker that we met near the beginning of this chapter, found, from sending out the questionnaires, that, on the whole, people in their 90s did not feel isolated, but that people in their 80s and 70s did (perhaps because people who make it to their 90s have very particular characteristics, such as determination or a positive mental attitude). It was also found that the feelings of isolation were associated with depression and ill health. On the basis of these results, the social worker successfully secured funding to set up a 'befriending' service. A bank of volunteers was established, who would visit older people in their own homes, or go out with them, for an hour or so each week. The social worker wants to evaluate this new service to see whether it does reduce people's feelings of isolation by determining whether:
1. People's sense of isolation has decreased (or not).
2. If a decrease is shown, whether it is due to the befriending service.
3. The decrease is a *real*, or *significant* decrease, or whether it is just a chance finding that is it is more likely to be due to a cocktail of other unrelated factors.

Numbers 1 and 2 can be answered by using the isolation scale referred to earlier, with a group of older people before and then after they have the befriending service and by comparing their results with a control group of people who do not get the service. Answering number 3 is where *statistical tests, analyses* or *techniques* come in.

All three terms mean largely the same thing and all three are *tools*. Statistical tests are just tools. For example, if you wanted to know how long a piece of string was, a ruler might be the tool of choice; if you needed to find out the temperature in a room, a thermometer would be a handy tool; if you were assessing the anxiety level of a particular client, you could use, as a tool, a standardised anxiety scale; if you wanted to know how independent Mrs Johns was, the Barthel Index might be a useful tool; if you needed to determine the support systems that Mr Gregg had at home, the Single Assessment Tool could help.

Statistical tests are tools that can tell us three things:

- Whether things are *different* (for example, is there a real difference between the depression scores of people who receive cognitive behavioural therapy and those who receive counselling?).
- Whether things are *related* (for example, are school exam results related to IQ?).
- Whether these differences or associations are just chance occurrences.

For example, statistical tests can tell us whether the degree of independence of young people with a learning disability who live in supported housing is significantly *different* than the degree of independence of young people with a learning disability who live at home. Statistical tests can also tell us whether the likelihood of children having depression is significantly *related* to one of their parents being severely depressed.

Significantly is the key word here. Statistical tests can answer questions about whether things are different or about whether things are related, and they can tell us if these differences or associations are *statistically significant*.

Statistical significance: What's that all about?

The social worker evaluating the befriending scheme referred to above arranges for 50 people in their 70s and 80s to be visited by a volunteer (the intervention group). All 50 are asked to rate their degree of isolation before they have the scheme and then again three months after. There are 50 other people on a waiting list for the scheme. Their self-ratings of isolation are also taken at the same time points (but they do not get the befriending scheme yet since they are to act as a control group). The mean isolation scores at baseline were as follows: 23 for the people in the befriending group, 25 for those in the control group. After the intervention, the mean score in the befriending group had gone up to 62, whilst the mean score of the people in the control group was 34. These statistics might lead you to conclude that the befriending scheme did seem to be doing the trick (because the scores of the people who had it improved *more* than the scores of the people who did not). However, how can we tell whether this is a *real* difference, and not just a chance finding? If the social worker (or someone else) did the evaluation again would they be likely to come to the same conclusion?

In the example outlined above, the scores changed as follows:

Intervention		Control
23	Baseline	25
↓		↓
62	Follow-up	34

What if they had changed like this instead?

Intervention		Control
23	Baseline	25
↓		↓
46	Follow-up	35

Or, like this?

Intervention		Control
23	Baseline	25
↓		↓
39	Follow-up	37

Would you count these changes as *real* differences and still conclude that the befriending scheme had a significant effect on older people's sense of isolation? There needs to be some way of deciding what is a real or significant difference. This is where *statistical significance* can help.

Statistical significance is the probability that an observed difference could have arisen by chance. In this example, this would translate as 'the probability that the difference in isolation scores between the group who had the befriending service and the group who did not was due to chance'.

Statistical tests look at the data that have been collected (in this case, the isolation scores of all the older people in both groups at baseline and follow-up) and tell you what this probability is. (Different statistical tests answer different types of questions, but we will come back to this.) This probability is called the *p value*.

P values: What do they tell us?

The probability that a difference is due to chance, or *p* value, can range from 0 to 1:

- 0 means that there is very little possibility the difference in scores is due to chance.
- 1 means it is as certain as we can be that this difference is due to chance.

Some people find that Figure 4.6 helps illustrate what a *p* value means; some people find it makes the whole thing more confusing. Please take it or leave it as you find useful.

In descriptive terms, this is what a *p* value tells you. A statistical test might be run to see whether there is a statistically significant difference between the

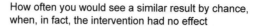

How often you would see a similar result by chance,
when, in fact, the intervention had no effect

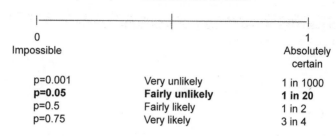

0		1
Impossible		Absolutely certain
p=0.001	Very unlikely	1 in 1000
p=0.05	**Fairly unlikely**	**1 in 20**
p=0.5	Fairly likely	1 in 2
p=0.75	Very likely	3 in 4

Figure 4.6   P values

number of times boys change foster carers and the number of times girls do. (This would require information to have been collected about the number of times lots of boys and lots of girls had changed foster carers, and if the boys and girls were similar in terms of age, family background, and so on.) The statistical test would look at all the data and come up with a probability, or p value. This p value would tell you the probability that any difference between the number of times that boys and the number of times that girls change foster carers is due to chance. If the p value turned out to be 0.75, this would mean that three out of four times the difference would be due to chance (so only one in four times it would be a real difference); if the p value was 0.1 this would mean that one in ten times the difference would be due to chance (so nine out of ten times it would be a real difference); or if p was 0.05 this would mean that one in 20 times the difference would be due to chance (and 19 out of 20 times it would be a real difference).

A p value of 0.05 might sound familiar. This is because a probability value of 0.05 is conventionally used as the cut-off to decide whether a finding is statistically significant or not. If a p value is 0.05 or less, this is taken to mean that the finding is statistically significant; there is a real difference. In the example above, if p was found to be 0.05 or less ($p \leq 0.05$), the conclusion would be drawn that there *is a difference* between the number of times girls and boys change foster carers. If p turned out to be *greater than 0.05* ($p > 0.05$ or ns – non-significant), the conclusion would be that there is *no difference* in the number of times that boys and girls change foster carers. In other words, we are saying if we were to get the same result by chance only one in 20 times this is good enough for us to conclude that it is a 'true' finding.

This p value of 0.05 is just an arbitrary cut-off, which has been traditionally used by statisticians. Sometimes, if researchers want to be more certain that a finding is a 'true' finding they will use the more stringent p value of 0.01 as their cut-off to decide whether a finding is statistically significant or not.

This means that only one in 100 times the result would be found by chance and 99 times out of 100 it would be a true difference.

The following is an example of how *p* values are reported in research papers. It is an extract from the *Buying Time* study [7], which was described in Chapter 3. In essence the aim of the work was to determine the effectiveness (and cost effectiveness) of a stay in a residential rehabilitation unit for older people (intervention group), as compared to 'usual' community services (control group). As this was a quasi-experimental study, it was important that the intervention and control groups were closely matched at baseline.

Overall there were no key differences between the intervention and control groups at baseline, although there were two statistically significant differences. More of the intervention group than the control group lived alone (intervention 67.0%, control 52.7%: $\chi^2 = 4.2$, df = 1, p = 0.041) and the intervention group was slightly older than the control group (mean [sd]: 83.1 [7.1] years and 80.7 [8.5] years, respectively; t = 2.2, df = 204 p = 0.028).

Risk assessments: the risk of risks

Risk is normally understood to mean the probability that a particular adverse event will occur. Research studies often report results based on the use of screening or assessment instruments; most commonly this will comprise a statistic indicating how common a phenomenon is in the population being studied. The statistic will often then be used to predict prevalence in a general population. We described how sensitivity and specificity are important attributes of literature search strategies in Chapter 2. In relation to predictive assessments of diagnostic tests, sensitivity refers to how good a test or an assessment is at correctly identifying a person at risk ('true positives'). Specificity, on the other hand, refers to how good a test or assessment is at identifying those who are *not* at risk ('true negatives'). As with literature searches, assessments or tests need to perform well on both dimensions in order to be of much use to us. Crucially, the sensitivity and specificity of tests or assessments also vary depending on whether the test is used on a population already known to be 'at risk' or an unscreened general population. This is because we would expect to encounter a higher proportion of problems in the 'at risk' population than in a random population sample. For example, the sensitivity and specificity of a screening instrument used in an A&E department to detect whether a child has been sexually abused would vary, depending on whether the instrument is used just for children *already* on a child protection register, or with *all* children who present at A&E. We would expect, in this example, far more false positive diagnoses in the latter case.

The danger of failing to factor false positives into our calculations can be illustrated by a statistical example. A risk assessment instrument, designed to predict the suicide risk of discharged psychiatric patients, which has 80 per cent sensitivity (ability to locate true positives) and 80 per cent specificity (ability to locate true negatives) would identify, given the known rate of suicides in the period after discharge, 32 true positives and almost 4,000 false ones [8]. Even when – unlike suicide, the prevalence of a problem is relatively high, for example, 10 per cent – a screening instrument of 80 per cent specificity and sensitivity will misdiagnose twice as many people as it diagnoses correctly [9]. Although false positives are likely to be fewer where a phenomenon is more common and confined to very specific and easily identifiable population groups, social welfare interventions are often con-cerned with comparatively rare events. For example, infant homicides occur roughly 10 times per 200,000 live births in England and Wales. If we screened all parents of newborn children with an instrument designed to identify the perpetrators of infant homicide of 90 per cent specificity and sensitivity, the chance of any positive result being 'true' would be 0.0002 per cent [10]. When reading the results of studies which include screening or assessment instruments, we need to ensure that first, the sensitivity and specificity of the instrument has been reported and second, that the instrument was being used on the population for which it was designed.

The prior knowledge that any experienced social worker is likely to have about the likelihood of encountering a particular problem within a given population is normally unaccounted for in traditional approaches to statistical calculations. Statisticians tend to fall into two camps; 'frequentists' and 'Bayesians', with the former being, until recently, far more numerous and influential [11]. The Reverend Thomas Bayes (1702–1761) addressed this sampling and prediction problem 270 years ago, although it is only recently, largely due to the exponential increase in computing power, that the 'Bayesian' approach has become more prominent. Bayes' Theorem deals with assessing risks from what is known generally at the time of estimating them, but then suggests that these risks should be adjusted in the light of later information [10]. The Bayesian approach has much to offer to those working within social care services as, unlike the frequentist approach, it enables our prior knowledge about the population being studied – the *prior distribution* – being factored into the calculations. Any modification to this prediction resulting from the data subsequently collected is known as the posterior distribution. This means, simply, that our prior beliefs about the nature of a problem are modified with actual information. For example, imagine that 'known to have done it before' was added to a list of child abuse risk factors. This would result in a change to our prior calculation of the odds of an event happening, which may – or may not – be supported by subsequent data. The relevance of a Bayesian approach to evidence-based practice is that it enables us to test our prior assumptions and amend them – or not – as new information emerges.[1]

Inter-rater reliability – the kappa statistic

One opinion is good, two opinions are better. The kappa statistic – represented by the symbol κ – is a measure of agreement between two or more parties. It is very useful for estimating the extent to which several people agree about some aspect of data where confirmatory opinions are required. This is especially relevant where a degree of judgement is required as to whether, for example, a study meets or does not meet pre-set eligibility criteria for a review, or in which of several categories statements or views should be placed. The kappa statistic ranges from 0 (no agreement at all) to 1 (perfect agreement) [12]. Scores between 0–0.2 are usually described as having only slight agreement, 0.3–0.4 fair, 0.5–0.6 moderate, 0.7–0.8 substantial and above 0.8 almost perfect. The following example is based on a recent study by one of the authors in South Wales [13].

Children's wishes

A questionnaire was distributed in junior schools by the children's teachers and collected when complete. It asked, 'if you had one wish, what would it be?' No names or identifying details were requested. An analytical structure was devised, with 11 categories. The wishes were detached from the child's personal details and the code assignment done blind to the age and gender of the child by the study author. To check whether the category assignment would be replicated by a second person, a randomly selected sample of 70 wishes, plus the coding schedule, was sent to a colleague, who assigned codes without consultation. Inter-rater reliability was high ($\kappa = 0.71$). The main conclusion was related to gender. There was a significant relationship between wishes associated with power and boys, and an even stronger relationship between wishes associated with affiliation and girls, confirming the strength of gender stereotypes.

If no such confirmation had taken place, we would have to rely on a single person's opinion. As the views of two people independently concurred, we

---

[1] Further details of the relevance of Bayes' theorem to social work practice can be found at *http://turnbull.mcs.st-and.ac.uk/history/Mathematicians/Bayes.html*

can have more confidence that the assignments are valid. The added protection of blind assignment also means that we can be fairly sure that the findings related to gender are unbiased.

Which statistical analysis for which questions?

We have now covered the main statistical concepts that the evidence-based practitioner needs to grasp in order to understand the results section of a quantitative research paper. You do not need to have an in-depth under-standing of how statistical significance or a *p* value is calculated. It is enough to know the use that these pieces of information have in order to be able to interpret and critically appraise a results section. It would also help to have a framework of some of the statistical tests most commonly encountered.

We have described statistical tests divided into those that look to see if there are significant *differences* and those which determine whether there are significant *associations*. We will continue with this categorisation.

Differences

Before we look at the types of analysis that are most commonly used to test for differences in social care research reports and papers, it is worth taking a moment to think about *how* this sort of information should be analysed.

With a pre-post study, the aim is to see whether something has significantly improved after an intervention. The researcher is looking for a difference in scores/numbers/frequencies between baseline and the end of the interven-tion. For example, a family resource centre is set up. One of its primary aims is to improve the behaviour of young children. The behaviour of children is measured, using a validated scale when they first visit the centre and again after they have been coming for six months. The researchers should analyse the data to see whether the scores at follow up are *statistically significantly* different (hopefully, improved) from the scores at baseline.

However, as discussed in detail in the critical appraisal chapter, a pre-post study always leaves in the air the question of whether any difference, or improvement, is really due to the intervention, or whether it is due to other factors at play (for example, the passage of time). As we have seen in Chapter 3, the way to be more certain that any difference is due to the intervention and not these other things is to run a quasi-experimental study, or a randomised controlled trial. Again, this would mean using the validated scale at baseline and follow up, but also having a control group of children whose scores are measured but who do not go to the family resource centre. What the researchers are then looking for is whether the scores of the children who go to the centre have *improved more* than the scores of the children in the control group. This means working out (or getting a statistics package to work out) how much each child's score has improved (or got worse, as the case may be) from baseline to follow up, and then comparing the *amounts of change* between the intervention and control groups.

You might come across quasi-experimental studies which only compare the follow-up scores of the two groups. This is an incorrect way of comparing outcomes, and means there was no point taking baseline scores. You might also read reports of RCTs which just look to see the amount of change in the intervention group. What then was the point of having a control group? Doing the analysis like this means the researchers might as well have done a pre-post study. The data in quasi-experimental studies and RCTs should be analysed by comparing the amount of *change* in the intervention group with the amount of *change* in the control group to see whether they are *statistically significantly different*.

The statistical test used to compare sets of scores to see if they are significantly different depends on the type of data collected. As a rule of thumb, if it is appropriate to report *mean* scores, so called *parametric tests* can be used, one of the most common of which is the *t-test*. If it is not okay to report mean scores, and the median is reported instead, then so-called non-parametric tests should be used, the two most common of which are the *Mann-Whitney U test* and the *Wilcoxon signed-ranks test*.

The following extract shows how the results of statistical tests might be reported in research papers:

The length of time in hospital at baseline was statistically significantly different between the two groups. Those in the intervention group stayed a mean (sd) of 31.6 (16.4) days and the controls a mean (sd) of 40.6 (28.3) days. This equated to a median (IQR) of 27 (20) days for the intervention group and a median (IQR) of 35 (25) days for the control group (U = 4234, p = 0.029).

Associations

If a piece of research is looking to see whether factor X is related to factor Y, statistical tests of association are used. For example, if a researcher wanted to investigate whether the degree of independence of people with physical disabilities is associated with the severity of their disability, or if there is an association between job satisfaction and the size of social work teams, they could use a *chi-squared test* (χ^2) or a *correlation coefficient* to statistically test for associations.

Chi-squared tests are used when information is in categories. For example, at the Centre for Evidence-Based Social Services (CEBSS), we carried out a survey involving 2,315 professional-grade social care staff, which asked about their views and knowledge of evidence-based practice. One of the aims of the survey was to see whether people who have attended CEBSS' events or read our publications had a better grasp of the meaning of research terms. For example, data were analysed to determine whether there was a statistically significant association between people's attendance at our events and whether they could correctly identify the main features of a randomised controlled trial. A chi-squared test was used to see if there was a statistically significant association. (By the way, the answer was 'yes'; $\chi^2 = 8.7$, $df = 2$, $p < 0.05$. See [14] for further results of this survey.)

In terms of associations, *Pearson's r* is used when it is appropriate to report the data as means, and *Spearman's rank correlation coefficient* when it should be reported as medians. (An excellent book [3] gives a much fuller introductory description of the appropriateness and application of these and other statistical tests.)

Remind me . . . Why is all this relevant to me as an evidence-based social worker?

Within this chapter we hope to have given three main messages:

- Statistics are pieces of numerical information that only have value if they have meaning, are useful, or useable.
- There is a difference between statistics *per se* and statistical tests.
- Statistical tests are just tools to answer questions.

This all becomes relevant when the questions that the statistical tests help answer relate to your client or practice decision making. For example, if you were working with clients with learning disabilities and challenging behaviour, a research report that has investigated the effectiveness of a one-to-one programme for managing challenging behaviour might be relevant. You get a copy of the report to see whether it is. The first thing we hope that this chapter has achieved is that you will now look through the results section of the report and not feel so mystified by the jargon, or so overwhelmed by the terminology, that you put it to one side. As a critical appraiser, there are then two main things you need to know:

1. Is it relevant to my clients?
2. Is it trustworthy?

Relevance. Understanding about the three types of average and measures of spread, will help you make a judgement about whether the clients who took part in the study are similar enough to your clients for you to feel happy about using the results in your decision making. You can get this information if the results section clearly describes the people who took part.

Trustworthiness. You will only be able to judge the trustworthiness of the piece of research, or be able to come to a conclusion about whether you are sure enough of its quality to use it in your decision making, if you have a grasp of what is given in the results section. This does not depend on understanding the ins and outs of any terminology or jargon. It is much more dependent on looking through the results with a critical eye and thinking about some of the following:

- Was it right to report means, or should medians have been given?
- Were standard deviations reported when inter-quartile ranges would have been more appropriate?
- Was the statistical significance of the study findings given? If so, what were the *p* values? What do these *p* values mean?
- Were the data analysed in the right sort of way? For example, were the amounts of *change* compared between the intervention and control groups in a quasi-experimental study?
- Were the right sort of statistical tests used? For example, was a t-test used when it was not appropriate to report means?
- Do the results tally with the conclusions? For example, do the authors claim things other than what they have shown in their results?

(Further details are given in a very helpful paper in the *British Journal of Social Work* [15].)

If a number of the above are not clear from the paper, or the answers to these questions give you cause for concern, you may decide that the research is not trustworthy enough and that you do not feel happy using it to inform your decision making. This is at the heart of social work practice; only using pieces of information or evidence that are good quality, so that you know the decisions made between you and your client are based on the best available evidence.

Acknowledgement

We would like to thank all the social care staff who have attended our 'Appraising the Evidence' training and have helped us take a step closer to putting this chapter into plain English.

References

[1] Blaise Pascal, 1662, cited in Bernstein, P.L. (1998) *Against the Gods: The Remarkable Story of Risk*. New York: John Wiley and Sons.

[2] Weinbach, R.W. and Grinnell, R.M. (2001) *Statistics for Social Workers*. 5th edn. Boston, MA: Allyn and Bacon.

[3] For a fuller explanation, we recommend: Greene, J. and D'Oliveria, M. (2001) *Learning to Use Statistical Tests in Psychology*. 2nd edn. Buckingham: Open University Press.

[4] *www.phru.nhs.uk/casp/casp.htm*. Accessed on 19.04.04.

[5] Bowers, D. (1996) *Statistics from Scratch*. Chicester: John Wiley & Sons.

[6] *http://www.dh.gov.uk/PolicyAndGuidance/OrganisationPolicy/TertiaryCare/DelayedDischarge/fs/en.* Accessed on 19.04.04.

[7] Trappes-Lomax, T., Ellis, A. and Fox, M. (2002) *Buying Time. An Evaluation and Cost Effectiveness Analysis of a Joint Health/Social Care Residential Rehabilitation Unit for Older People on Discharge From Hospital.* Centre for Evidence-Based Social Services; University of Exeter.

[8] Geddes, J. (1999) Suicide and homicide by people with mental illness. *British Medical Journal.* 318: 1225–6.

[9] Clark, A. and Harrington, R. (1999). On diagnosing rare disorders rarely: appropriate use of screening instruments. *Journal of Child Psychology and Psychiatry.* 40: 2, 287–90.

[10] MacDonald, K.J. and MacDonald, G.M. (1999) Perceptions of risk. In Parsloe, P. (Ed.) *Risk Assessment in Social Care and Social Work.* Research Highlights in Social Work 36. London: Jessica Kingsley.

[11] Bland, J.M. and Altman, D.G. (1998) Bayesians and Frequentists. *British Medical Journal.* 317: 1151.

[12] Fink, A. (1998) *Conducting Research Literature Reviews: From Paper to the Internet.* London: Sage.

[13] Newman, T. (in press, 2004) Money, friends and muscles: the wishes of primary schoolchildren in a South Wales community. *Research, Policy and Planning.* 22, 3.

[14] Sheldon, B., Chilvers, R., Ellis, A., Moseley, A. and Tierney, S. (in press) An empirical study of obstacles to, and opportunities for, evidence-based practice in social care. In *Evidence-Based Practice and Social Work: International Research and Policy Perspectives.* London: Whiting & Birch.

[15] Smeeton, N. and Goda, D. (2003) Conducting and presenting social work research: some basic statistical considerations. *British Journal of Social Work.* 33: 567–73.

Chapter 5

Service Users and Evidence-based Practice

This chapter discusses the role of service users within evidence-based practice as:
- Participants in research.
- Producers of research.
- Consumers of research.

> *'doption, sir, is when folks gets a girl to work without wages.*
> (Informant, female, aged 16–17, to Pauper Children (Canada) report,
> presented to the House of Commons, 8th February 1875)

Introduction

Evidence-based practice is often associated more with a 'doing to' rather than a 'doing with', let alone a 'doing on behalf of' approach to social care. The reasons for this are varied. Among the more important are a perception that the most valued kind of knowledge derives from clinical trials rather than personal testimony, which privileges those that can understand it and disempowers those that cannot; that a focus on outcomes diminishes the importance of process, especially in therapeutic relationships; and that service users are rarely placed in the driver's seat, and when they are, it is only on condition that they have a co-driver and L plates. These views cannot be casually dismissed. However, the perception of evidence-based practice as diminishing the user experience is, while understandable, very wide of the mark. Evidence-based practice can neither flourish nor survive without promoting and nurturing the role of users in all parts of research production. Without user involvement, we cannot make reliable judgements about what questions are significant, what kinds of services should be evaluated, and what kinds of outcomes really matter to people.

In recent years formalised user involvement has grown from being a marginal to a mainstream activity. As discussed below, this has resulted in the participation of service users not only as study informants, but also as producers and consumers of research. Underlying the current enthusiasm for user participation in service delivery and research is the hope that this will help to produce interventions that are acceptable and accessible to individuals, and which improve their quality of life.

Few readers will need persuading that the involvement of users in research production is a 'good thing'. In fact, placing the perspectives of users at the heart of social care services has become such a universal desiderata [1] that an increasingly important task is retaining a critical perspective, in being clear about what the benefits for clients should be, and when user involvement is more and less important. Therefore, within this chapter, some typical difficulties, as well as benefits, of user involvement and perspectives in social care research will be highlighted, to emphasise the need to retain a critical edge when approaching any investigation or source of knowledge. We may admire, for example, a study conceived, carried out and reported by a group of lone mothers living in poverty, but their deserved admiration does not, in itself, make the study any more accurate, reliable or useful. It is important to add that whilst a lot has been written about how to embed user involvement in service structures [2–4], the actual benefits of such involvement are still to be tested and supported via robust empirical studies.[1]

This chapter reflects on the central position service users play in evidence-based practice. It looks at service users as research participants, then as producers of research, and concludes by discussing how research can be utilised by people to make informed choices. However, before embarking on the different roles played within the research process by those receiving services, reasons for such involvement will be explored.

Reasons for service user involvement in research

User involvement in service evaluation and development in the UK has been shaped by a number of factors, all with powerful implications for the way social care research is conceived and pursued. Dimensions underlying the push for such participation include the following:

- *Defining agendas*. Some constituencies have demanded the right to define problems and solutions from their own perspective, rather than have these defined by professionals. 'Nothing about us without us' has become a rallying cry for a new generation of activists, who refuse to be treated as passive subjects of social or medical experimentation. The contribution made by this constituency to the utility of both social and medical research, by insisting that discriminatory attitudes and structures be considered by research designs, is transforming knowledge generation in this area, and is

---

[1] *www.scie.org.uk/publications/positionpapers/pp03.pdf* (checked on 27/07/04).

one of the most striking examples of how indispensable user views are to the research process.

- *Consumer choice.* A second thread sees users of social care services employing the same principles to assess the respective merits of welfare 'products' as we would to reach judgements about any other product the market makes available, such as price, utility, functionality, convenience, longevity, aesthetic attractiveness and so on. As consumers, individuals need to be able to compare and contrast services to reach informed decisions, which places a premium on accurate, impartial and accessible sources of information. Social care research thus has an important role to play in helping service users discriminate between different welfare 'products' and to choose the one that is right for them.

- *Professional decision making.* Decisions about the welfare of individuals, as well as broader decisions about strategic investment, can expect to be informed by material collected though a variety of avenues; surveys, whether by post, telephone or personal interview; focus groups; secondary analysis of existing data sets, such as client records, or the views of service users involved in planning forums. Collecting information from service users – current or potential, and from children as well as adults – about service options, service quality, or preferred investment choices, is a core task of social care research, and essential to the development of services that are relevant to people's needs.

- *Participatory democracy* – A final strand of user involvement relevant to social care research is the growing importance attached to participation as a vehicle for promoting more dynamic local democracy and the involvement of communities in social change. This may vary from discrete, time-limited projects to long term involvement in permanent decision making bodies. Direct user control of the research process, often employing an action research model, is an important feature of this dimension of user participation.

Service users as participants in research

Listening to the views of those on the receiving end of social welfare services has a long legacy. Almost three hundred years ago, a petition from the inmates of the Bedlam asylum was presented to the House of Lords complaining about cruel and inhumane treatment. Over a century ago, as illustrated in our opening quote, it was possible for children's views to be solicited and cited in parliamentary reports. Up to the early twentieth century, children who were proposed for intercontinental migration by Poor Law unions had first to appear before a magistrate and confirm that this was also their wish. More recently, client opinion studies have been embedded within welfare services. This has enabled us to gain an insight into the experiences of users, whose choices and values may differ from those who provide services. For example, clinicians may typically place greater importance than patients on the physical limitations associated with a degenerative illness, whereas patients tend to stress the importance of positive mental health and vitality [5]. Similarly, users of social care services have reported that the issues that really make a difference to their lives, such as assistance at home, or help to go shopping, have not been equally prioritised by professionals [6]. Family support services tend to focus on issues of behavioural change and emotional support, whereas families themselves may be more concerned about income support, education and childcare [7]. As these examples suggest, service users may employ a different set of calculations to that of professionals. Without exploring these perspectives, we are unlikely to offer the range of options that people really want, making the notion of informed choice impossible.

One way of exploring the views of service users is via a survey, as the following scenario illustrates:

A rehabilitation team is interested in evaluating the views of the older people they work with, in terms of the equipment provided to promote their independence. They therefore use an occupational therapy student on placement to carry out a client satisfaction survey as part of her final year dissertation. The student spends an hour with each person seen by the team, asking them a series of questions about the equipment. Each question is weighted to measure their satisfaction. Feedback from this survey enables the team to see which areas of their service are perceived as most and least helpful. Practitioners act upon responses accordingly.

Client opinion studies derive from a growing unwillingness to accept authoritarian views, and the realisation that service users' perspectives have always, albeit non-systematically, actively influenced professional decision making [8]. This has resulted in a plethora of qualitative investigations in social care, examining 'how was it for you?' type questions. However, while the quality of professional decision making is likely to improve when it is rooted in the perspectives of service users, challenges remain. For example, a focus on users' views may often emphasise the *quality* of the encounter with social welfare services, while paying less attention to the outcomes. In some cases, satisfaction or approval may be expressed by users for services or procedures which, overall, appear to do more harm than good. Examples of this are mass critical incident stress debriefing for witnesses of disasters or traumatic incidents, which may increase rather than decrease the overall burden of post-traumatic stress disorder [9]; programmes that teach young people safe driving habits, which may result in more rather than fewer accidents due to the programme's unintended outcome of increasing the number of young people who drive cars [10]; and universal screening for breast cancer, which may result in an increase in morbidity due to the resulting unnecessary removal of low grade or benign tumours [11].

A further problem relating to client opinion studies is the relative absence of the voices of those who do not constitute the existing service user population. Most of the information we have comes from people already engaged with services, making it difficult to examine the reasons why highly vulnerable sections of the community choose not to use, for example, a family support service. In relation to this point, the opinions of more vulnerable service users have previously been gained second hand from carers and providers. For instance, the proxy views of adults were utilised in the past to rate the respective importance of different life events to children [12]. As a consequence, transient, traumatic events were thought to be of greatest importance to youngsters. However, this is not what children tell us; from their perspective, being bullied, performing poorly at school, persistent parental conflict and having no friends loom larger than dramatic but essentially short-lived episodes [13]. The neglect of children's and adolescents' opinions within existing research has resulted in calls for young people to play a greater role in consultations and evaluations, so that their concerns and experiences are heard, and services provided in line with what they require [14].

The following scenario highlights the point:

Practitioners working in a Child and Adolescent Mental Health Service want to find out what their clients think of the assistance they provide. So, they carry out a series of one-to-one interviews with a random sample of young people seen there. They also decide to examine the opinions of parents of these youngsters, to see how far their views mirror or diverge from those of their children. They find some overlap in terms of qualities regarded as important in a therapist by the young people and their parents. However, the teenagers involved are far more disparaging of the family therapy they receive, stating that it is too difficult to speak about things in their parents' company. Conversely, parents report that this intervention is helpful because it gives them the opportunity to speak about the child and his/her mental health

problem in a mediated environment. This difference between the
children and their parents would have been lost if only parents – or
indeed, only children – were asked to speak about the service.

Consultation with other vulnerable individuals, such as people with learning
disabilities, has also become more common in recent years [15]; guidelines
about their involvement in research have been developed [16–17], and
methodological and practical issues have been discussed [18–20]. In addition,
ethical dilemmas associated with this type of research have been raised [21],
for example, the challenge of ensuring that people are equipped to make
informed choices, explaining the concepts of 'anonymity' and 'confidentiality'
[22], and investigating the views of those with severe disabilities in a
meaningful and respectful manner [23]. Developing relationships with vulnerable and often lonely people through research can be problematic, since these
relationships must inevitably end, and may leave some individuals feeling even
more isolated. In such circumstances, researchers should contemplate the
ending of a study carefully.

A final point to make in terms of service users as participants in research is
that they may volunteer to take part in a trial, which usually targets specific
population groups, often selected by age or gender. Indeed, this is an option
open to any of us. Users who wish to know more about trials should consult
the NHS National Electronic Library for Health website *www.nelh.nhs.uk/
clinicaltrials*. This website, developed in consultation with patients, is specifically designed for members of the public.

Service users as producers of research

One way of ensuring that evidence is sensitive to service users' needs is to
include them in the prioritisation and execution of research. The demand from
funding bodies for user involvement to have been demonstrated on grant
applications is a factor that has helped to promote the participation of service
users in the research process, with funders increasingly expecting to see
evidence that actual or potential clients have been, at the very least, consulted
about the value of a proposed study. The establishment of organisations such
as *Involve* has helped in this process. *Involve* (formerly Consumers in NHS
Research) was set up by the Director of R&D in the NHS in 1996, and has
extended its remit to include social care. It has produced several useful
resources to promote user participation in the research process, including
guidelines for those wishing to involve people receiving a service in the
planning and/or management of a study.[2]

---

[2] *www.invo.org.uk* (checked on 27/07/04).

The benefits of service user involvement in producing research

Professionals may think that they have a clear idea of service users' views and concerns, but empirical material suggests otherwise [24–26]. Likewise, people who have experienced a particular problem, or those living with a condition, have a different insight into their situation compared to independent researchers lacking firsthand experience of their field of enquiry [27]. Hence, those receiving a service, it is argued, can help to prevent research from being shaped by narrow academic or professional interests, bringing a fresh perspective to an investigation, and introducing issues overlooked in the past [28].

Why service users might get involved in producing research

Service users may get involved in producing a study for a number of reasons. They may wish:[3]

- To improve services, for themselves and others.
- To tell their story and to have their voice heard.
- To highlight problems they think need addressing, including gaps in our current knowledge of a condition/situation.
- To guarantee that research is being conducted in an ethical manner.
- To know how research will be used once completed, and to make sure that findings are disseminated to those using services.

Engaging service users in the dissemination of research can be advantageous. They may have ideas about various networks and publications that could be used to ensure a wide distribution of a study's findings. Traditional dissemination routes are often limited in scope, with papers published in peer-reviewed journals, or delivered at a conference, only reaching a handful of researchers and practitioners, leaving many other professionals, service users and carers ignorant about an investigation. Methods of sharing research promoted through consumer involvement have included newsletters, websites, and presentations at support groups [29], with results delivered by service users themselves that are accessible and acceptable to those whose care might be affected by them.

To illustrate this point about dissemination, imagine that a team of researchers acquired some funding to carry out a randomised controlled trial comparing the outcome of individuals with a visual impairment receiving direct payments compared to those who do not. As part of their funding

---

[3] Adapted from *www.invo.org.uk/pdf/guide_for_consumers.pdf* (checked on 27/07/04).

application, these researchers specified that service users would be consulted about the project. From the outset of the study, three client representatives were involved as part of the research team. As well as advising on the approach taken to the investigation, and helping with the analysis, these individuals were able to disseminate its findings at service user groups, meetings and conferences, and to the 'talking newspaper association'.[4] They were also able to advise on how best to produce findings in formats accessible to those with visual difficulties.

Levels of involvement

Involvement in producing a piece of research does not mean that service users have to play a part at every stage of an investigation. Different levels of participation have been identified, from consultation, to collaboration, through to control.[5] Researchers might hold a single meeting with consumer representatives, asking for their ideas about priorities for a study. Alternatively, consumers might sit on a steering group for an investigation, and/or work with researchers on the design of a project, and/or help with the circulation of its findings. For example, a research team looking at the effectiveness of a programme to help homeless young people find accommodation contact a local organisation involved in assisting such individuals, to advertise for volunteers willing to sit on the project's steering group. Two young people agree to undertake this role and act in an advisory capacity on the issue of recruitment. However, they do not get involved in devising the methodology for the study, collecting data, analysing information, or writing up the results.

A third level of involvement is so-called 'user-led' research, in which a study is managed by service users, with professionals 'invited' to assist in the process. An example of such work includes *Strategies for Living* [30], a qualitative enquiry developed and carried out by individuals with mental health problems. Likewise, people with HIV/AIDS have designed and managed randomised controlled trials, examining the effectiveness of interventions for this condition.[6]

Despite a growing awareness of the importance of user participation in the execution of both social care and health research, it is still a marginal activity. A random sample of 1,000 NHS research projects found only 17 per cent with any degree of user involvement, and in most cases, this was very limited [31].

---

[4] This organisation provides national and local newspapers and magazines on audio tape, computer disk, e-mail, the internet and CD-ROM for visually impaired people (*www.tnauk.org.uk* checked on 27/07/04).

[5] *www.invo.org.uk/pdf/Briefing%20Note%20Final.dat.pdf* (checked on 27/07/04).

[6] *www.invo.org.uk/pdf/guide_for_consumers.pdf* (checked on 27/07/04).

Researchers may resist involving service users in developing and conducting a study, believing that they have little to contribute to this endeavour. However, although service users may not be experts in methodology, they can make valuable comments and observations about the design of an enquiry and the relative importance of the question it is trying to answer [32]. Another objection sometimes raised against such participation in research is that service users might approach the process in a partial, non-scientific manner. In defence of such a charge, others have stressed that users are not the only people with a vested interest in a study's findings. For example, practitioners may have a long term commitment to a specific approach; researchers may be reluctant to accept findings that deviate from their personal beliefs, or they may be compromised by the activities of their funding source. Even where such partiality exists, the views of those receiving a service can help to redress this balance [33].

An additional argument against the participation of users in research planning and execution is that those involved in such a venture become 'professionalised' and, therefore, lose their status as a service user. However, service users who contribute to the production of a study may be those most confident about challenging academics' perspectives of a situation, having built up a sufficient reservoir of skills and knowledge.

Considerations for involving service users in the production of research

Involving service users in the production of research may mean that attention has to be paid to logistical considerations, such as access requirements, facilitators, and interpreters, all of which cost money and take time to organise. In addition, user groups have raised the issue of remuneration, arguing that service users taking part in a study should receive payment for such an activity, to reflect the transfer of knowledge and value of their input [34]. It is also essential to acknowledge that some service users may be unaccustomed to voicing their opinions, requiring the opportunity to put forward their views at their own pace. Participative work, therefore, can take time and money, clashing with deadlines and financial limitations associated with research.

Problems reported by researchers who have tried involving service users in projects include the presence of an individual's practitioner as part of a research team, recruiting those who are articulate and confident but then wondering about their representativeness, and the fact that people who have had an adverse experience of services are often attracted to take part in projects, which can result in an 'us and them' situation [35]. Researchers are advised to bear these challenges in mind, whilst also being aware that service user involvement in research production can result in a more rounded array of opinions and concerns being addressed, and relevant outcomes being assessed [36].

The involvement of service users in an enquiry can be an empowering experience, in which these individuals are no longer regarded as passive subjects, but become part of the research team, helping to define priorities and to formulate questions, to collect data and also to analyse the information gathered.[7] However, care should be taken so that such involvement is not tokenistic, with service users simply there to fulfil a funding body's requirement.

It is important to consider that user groups may typically favour qualitative over quantitative research approaches, which are not, as discussed in Chapter 3, always the best means of investigating certain social problems and answering particular questions, especially questions about whether particular services or interventions work or not. Finally, user groups – like professional constituencies – may be uncomfortable with results that challenge preconceived opinions.

Service users as consumers of research

An enormously encouraging development over the past few decades in both health and social care research has been the growing need to justify research investment on the grounds of what benefit can be expected to accrue to the end user – the client or patient. This links to the issue of service users as consumers of research.

For evidence-based practice to achieve its potential, service users need to engage in the process, which can help to improve collaborative decision making between those receiving and those providing a service. Those who use services offered by social care professionals have a right to know on what basis decisions affecting their lives have been made. By being clear about the research base underpinning these decisions, practitioners can explain to clients why such an approach is being taken [37].

While social care practice may have led in the development of participatory strategies, health care research has been far more active in producing resources that enable patients to exercise informed choice. Before engaging in a dialogue with a physician over many common ailments, a health service user is able to examine the research base to see how well different treatment options are supported, and is thus better equipped to reach a joint decision

---

[7] *www.ccnap.org.uk/InvolvingPeople/theguide.htm* (checked on 27/07/04).

about the specific approach that is best for them. This can have positive outcomes for patients. For example, women with breast cancer have been reported to be less depressed and anxious if treated by a doctor who is open about their case and its treatment during consultations [38]. Similarly, individuals with diabetes, it is suggested, manage their condition better if able to engage in active discussions with professionals about their care [39]. However, there are some exceptions. For example, we are warned that children with cancer who are intimately involved in the details of their treatment plans may become more depressed than children who are less involved [40]. Therefore, as noted above, as well as any benefits arising from the process, we need to pay attention to the *outcomes* of participation, and not make the *a priori* assumption that participation, in all cases, and in all circumstances is a good thing.

In order to make an informed choice, those who have an elective rather than a mandatory relationship with services should be provided with sufficient material about the respective merits of different options, between which it is possible to discriminate meaningfully. Clearly, where these conditions are not present, the notion of the user as 'consumer' remains an aspiration rather than a reality.

Practitioners considering producing information for service users about their care might wish to consider the following [41]:

- Keep in mind the purpose of the information, and the proposed audience.
- Assess the available literature, basing any information on the most robust, current research, and be clear about the strength of any evidence referred to within the document.
- Plan in advance how you propose to distribute the material, and in what format.
- Think about occasional reviews and updating of information.
- Be honest about the benefits and risks of any suggested interventions.
- Include references for further information.
- Make sure the material is written in a clear and concise manner.

To bring this idea of producing information for service users to life, imagine that you work for a mental health team that assists people affected by schizophrenia. You and your colleagues agree that it is important to provide service users with leaflets about the effectiveness of different medications and psychosocial interventions (and to warn of potential side effects), so they are informed about the care they receive. Your team decides to draft some guidelines, summarising the best available evidence (from systematic reviews, or good quality RCTs). A group of your colleagues volunteer to undertake this task, and feel it is important that the material they produce is shaped by the needs and views of the intended audience. Consequently, they ask some service user representatives to assist them with the production of the leaflet, to ensure points are covered that they would expect to see in such a document and that it is written in an appropriate and accessible manner.

Apart from accessing ready-made information, service users may wish to search for evidence about their care themselves, an activity that has been facilitated by advances in information technology. Service users searching for evidence relevant to their situation will probably encounter similar difficulties to those experienced by practitioners attempting to locate data, one of the biggest being an excess rather than a paucity of information. As more and more resources become available online, valuable nuggets of information may be awash within a mass of irrelevant material. Strategies for overcoming this difficulty are described in Chapter 2; it may be advisable to pass on to service users interested in locating good quality evidence relating to their situation the information contained within this chapter.

It is important to note at this point that while relevant, high quality research may be available online, some of it is not free of charge, with e-journals and databases often requiring a subscription and password before they can be accessed. In addition, affording the equipment required to browse the internet could act as a barrier to equitable retrieval of online evidence-based information, although libraries now have computer terminals that can be used by the public, and initiatives are being piloted by the UK government to improve the accessibility of electronic information.

For service users to employ research that they retrieve in a discriminating manner, with an appropriate understanding, they need training not only in accessing, but also in critically appraising research. Imagine the following scenario:

After a stimulating course in how to read a piece of research in a critical manner, which covered the issues raised in Chapter 3 of this book, a service user advocate decides it is important that the information she has learnt is shared with other service users. She therefore sets up a series of workshops designed to teach service users about the trustworthiness and appropriateness of different pieces of research. From this initial event, a few people attending the course decide that this is an empowering activity, which needs to be shared more widely. After going to a patient and public involvement workshop, provided by the Public Health Resource Unit,[8] which

[8] *www.phru.nhs.uk/casp/workshopsPPI.htm* (checked on 27/07/04).

included further information about appraising and presenting evidence, these service users feel confident enough to deliver the training themselves, to other local service users.

Conclusion

In more recent times, involvement of clients in all aspects of research has changed the position of service users from that of subjects, to that of participants in studies and producers of information. This shift reflects a change from 'doing to' to 'doing with' clients, which as suggested in Chapter 1, is an important feature of evidence-based practice. However, for true partnership to flourish, service users must be provided with appropriate information, or be supported in searching for and appraising material themselves, so that knowledge is no longer the sole preserve of professionals.

It has been noted that while service user participation in research is increasing, there is a paucity of experimental enquiry examining the pros and cons of different approaches or strong evidence supporting the benefits of users' involvement in steering service provision. Despite the increasing popularity of user involvement, little robust investigation has been made of its advantages, or the best means of ensuring that the presence of service users is productive. It is suggested that such participation will progress best if attempts at service user involvement in service delivery and evaluation are fully documented, so that others can draw on and learn from these efforts [42].

References

[1] Hasler, F. (2003) *Users at the Heart: User Participation in The Governance and Operations of Social Care Regulatory Bodies*. SCIE Report No. 5. London: Social Care Institute for Excellence.

[2] Mordey, M. and Crutchfield, J. (2004) User involvement in supported housing: more than just ticking the box. *Housing Care and Support*. 7: 1, 7–10.

[3] Newman, J., Barnes, M., Sullivan, H. and Knops, A. (2004) Public participation and collaborative governance. *Journal of Social Policy*. 33:2, 203–23.

[4] Perkins, R. and Goddard, K. (2004) Reality out of the rhetoric: increasing user involvement in a mental health trust. *Mental Health Review*. 9:1, 21–24.

[5] Rothwell, P., Mcdowell, Z., Wong, C. and Dorman, P. (1997) Doctors and patients don't agree: cross-sectional study of doctor's and patient's perceptions and assessments of disability in multiple sclerosis. *British Medical Journal*. 314, 1580.

[6] Shaping Our Lives National User Network (2003) *Shaping Our Lives: What People Think of The Social Care Services They Use*. York: Joseph Rowntree Foundation.

[7] Penn, H. and Gough, D. (2002) The price of a loaf of bread: some conceptions of family support. *Children and Society*. 16, 17–32.

[8] Sainsbury, E. (1987) Client studies: their contribution and limitations in influencing social work practice. *British Journal of Social Work*. 17, 635–44.

[9] Bisson, J.I., Jenkins, P.L., Alexander, J. and Bannister, C. (1997) Randomized controlled trial of psychological debriefing for victims of acute burn trauma. *British Journal of Psychiatry*. 171, 78–81.

[10] Achara, S., Adeyemi, B., Dosekun, E. (The Cochrane Injuries Group Driver Education Reviewers) (2001) Evidence based road safety: the driving standards agency's schools programme. *The Lancet*. 358, 230–2.

[11] Olsen, O. and Gotzsche, P. (2001) Cochrane review on screening for breast cancer with mammography. *The Lancet*. 358, 1340–2.

[12] Coddington, R. (1972) The significance of life events as etiologic factors in the diseases of children: a survey of professional workers. *Journal of Psychosomatic Research*. 16, 7–18.

[13] Graham, P. (1994) Prevention. In Rutter, M., Taylor, E. and Hersov, L. (Eds.) *Child and Adolescent Psychiatry: Modern Approaches*. Oxford: Blackwell Scientific Publications.

[14] Moules, T. (2002) A case for involving children/young people in clinical audit. *British Journal of Clinical Governance*. 7:2, 86–91.

[15] Arscott, K., Dagnan, D. and Stenfert Kroese, B. (1998) Consent to psychological research by people with an intellectual disability. *Journal of Applied Research in Intellectual Disability*. 99:1, 77–83.

[16] Stalker, K. (1998) Some ethical and methodological issues in research with people with learning disabilities. *Disability and Society*. 13:1, 5–19.

[17] Swain, J., Heyman, B. and Gillman, M. (1998) Public research, private concerns: ethical issues in the use of open-ended interviews with people who have learning disabilities. *Disability and Society*. 13:1, 21–36.

[18] Atkinson, D. (1989) Research interviews with people with mental handicaps. In Brechin, A. and Walmsley, J. (Eds.) *Making Connections*. London: Hodder and Stoughton.

[19] Bond, J. (1999) Quality of life for people with dementia: approaches to the challenge of measurement. *Ageing and Society*. 19, 561–79;

[20] Booth, T. and Booth, W. (1994) *Parenting Under Pressure: Mothers and Fathers With Learning Disabilities*. Buckingham: Open University Press.

[21] Reid, D., Ryan, T. and Enderby, P. (2001) What does it mean to listen to people with dementia? *Disability and Society*.16:3, 377–92.

[22] McCarthy, M. (1998) Interviewing people with learning disabilities about sensitive topics: a discussion of ethical issues. *British Journal of Learning Disabilities*. 26, 140–45.

[23] Telford, R., Beverley, C.A., Cooper, C.L. and Boote, J.D. (2002) Consumer involvement in health research: fact or fiction? *British Journal of Clinical Governance*. 7:2, 92–103.

[24] Coulter, A., Peto, V. and Doll, H. (1994) Patients' preferences and general practitioners' decisions in the treatment of menstrual disorders. *Family Practice*.11, 67–74.

[25] Frater, A. (1992) Health outcomes: a challenge to the status quo. *Quality in Health Care*. 1, 87–88.

[26] Hares, T., Spencer, J., Gallagher, M., Bradshaw, C., and Webb, I. (1992) Diabetes care: who are the experts? *Quality in Health Care*. 1, 219–24.

[27] Entwistle, V.A., Renfrew, M.J., Yearley, S., Forrester, J. and Lamont, T. (1998) Lay perspectives: advantages for health research. *British Medical Journal*. 316, 463–67.

[28] Trivedi, P. and Wykes, T. (2002) From passive subjects to equal partners: qualitative review of user involvement in research. *British Journal of Psychiatry*. 181, 468–72.

[29] Trivedi, P. and Wykes, T. (2002) From passive subjects to equal partners: qualitative review of user involvement in research. *British Journal of Psychiatry*. 181, 468–72.

[30] Faulkner, A. (2000) *Strategies for Living: A Report of User-Led Research Into People's Strategies for Living With Mental Distress*. London: The Mental Health Foundation.

[31] Telford, R., Boote, J., Cooper, C. and Stobbs, M. (2003) *Principles of Successful Consumer Involvement in NHS Research: Results of a Consensus Study and National Survey. www.shef.ac.uk/content/1/c6/02/13/67/consumerssummary.pdf* (checked 21/1/05).

[32] for an Example See Trivedi, P. and Wykes, T. (2002) From passive subjects to equal partners: qualitative review of user involvement in research. *British Journal of Psychiatry*. 181, 468–72.

[33] Entwistle, V.A., Renfrew, M.J., Yearley, S., Forrester, J. and Lamont, T. (1998) Lay perspectives: advantages for health research. British Medical Journal. 316, 463–67.

[34] Consumers in NHS Research (2002) *A Guide to Paying Consumers Actively Involved in Research*. Hampshire: Consumers in NHS Research Support Unit.

[35] Telford, R., Beverley, C.A., Cooper, C.L. and Boote, J.D. (2002) Consumer involvement in health research: fact or fiction? *British Journal of Clinical Governance*. 7:2, 92–103.

[36] Trivedi, P. and Wykes, T. (2002) From passive subjects to equal partners: qualitative review of user involvement in research. *British Journal of Psychiatry*. 181, 468–72.

[37] Gambrill, E. (1997) *Social Work Practice: A Critical Thinker's Guide*. New York; Oxford: Oxford University Press.

[38] Fallowfield, L.J., Hall, A., Maguire, G.P. and Baum, M. (1990) Psychological outcomes of different treatment policies in women with early breast cancer outside a clinical trial. *British Medical Journal*. 301, 575–80.

[39] Kaplan, S.H., Greenfield, S. and Ware, J.E. (1989) Assessing the effects of physician-patient interactions on the outcomes of chronic disease. *Medical Care*. 27, S110–127.

[40] Phipps, S. and Srivastava, D. (1997) Repressive adaptation in children with cancer: it may be better not to know. *Journal of Pediatrics*.130, 257–65.

[41] Coulter, A., Entwistle, V. and Gilbert, D. (1999) Sharing decisions with patients: is the information good enough? *British Medical Journal*. 318, 318–22.

[42] Entwistle, V.A., Renfrew, M.J., Yearley, S., Forrester, J. and Lamont, T. (1998) Lay perspectives: advantages for health research. *British Medical Journal*. 316, 463–67.

Chapter 6

Staying Research Minded: Implementing Evidence-Based Practice

This chapter discusses:
- Applying research to practice.
- Obstacles to evidence-based practice.
- Increasing opportunities to access and read research.
- Increasing opportunities to discuss and reflect on research.
- Creating and sustaining an evidence-based culture in social care.

That is excellently observed . . . but let us dig in our garden [1].

Introduction

Previous chapters covered the steps of locating, making sense of, and appraising research. The final step in evidence-based practice, the process of implementing change based on messages from research, is perhaps the most challenging. Difficulties in applying research to practice can occur for a number of reasons. For example, the views and preferences of individual clients might contradict what research is telling us. Colleagues' views may differ still. As a practitioner you will therefore have to weigh up many sources of knowledge and claims to authority. In addition, it may be difficult to introduce certain interventions shown to be effective because of a lack of financial resources or specialist skills in your team or department. Sometimes you may feel you lack the authority or decision making power to act on the best available evidence. Other difficulties of application relate to the nature and type of evidence available. Evidence might not always be as robust as you would like, and it may not be entirely relevant to the case in hand. Furthermore, key differences may exist between the participants in a research study and the service users with whom you work.

In this book we do not want to oversimplify the process of evidence-based practice by assuming a straightforward, linear relationship between research and practice. Clearly there are a number of variables which affect social care practice, of which research is just one. In addition, there are a range of organisational or cultural factors which can either help or hinder evidence-based practice. In the first part of this chapter we discuss implementation issues and use worked examples to illustrate how research can inform practice. In the latter part we highlight obstacles to and enablers of evidence-based practice, and describe a number of straightforward, practical measures which can help us stay 'research minded' on a day-to-day basis and ensure research is kept high on the agenda within organisations. We use real life examples of activities carried out by social care practitioners with whom we have worked, and draw on the growing body of literature examining how to increase the influence of research on practice, implement research findings, and effectively disseminate research [2,3].

Applying research to practice

The nature of problems dealt with by social workers are complex and unpredictable in nature, requiring approaches which are tailored to suit individual circumstances. Practitioners need to use judgement and critical appraisal skills to decide whether research is relevant and applicable to the case in hand. As we noted in Chapter 3, research is only useful if it is both trustworthy *and* relevant. We acknowledged that the setting of a study might impact on its applicability to service users. For instance, if research had been conducted in the USA, would its findings be relevant in the UK? Additionally, the characteristics of the sample may be important. If a study had been carried out with people within a specific age range, would it be any use if the average age of our service users was different?

Using evidence can also be challenging since service users may require involvement from several agencies providing multiple interventions, resulting in the need for practitioners to have knowledge of research on a range of different topics, which can make acquisition of the relevant evidence seem like a heavy undertaking. The difficulties faced by some users may mean programmes are not completed and the client is therefore not exposed to the length or intensity of an intervention that may have proved successful in an experimental study. A practice situation will rarely be a perfect replica of a research study. However, few practitioners will encounter situations where the research base has nothing to offer. At best, it may highlight a new and well-attested procedure with which we were previously unfamiliar; at worst our knowledge base will improve and our critical faculties will be sharpened. In the section which follows we wish to demonstrate, using scenarios from different areas of social care, how well-constructed studies may offer new insights into our practice. While the research may not fit perfectly with the situations of all our clients, it can give us guiding principles about effective practice.

Case study 1: Education

Educational attainment is one of the most important factors associated with economic success in adult life. Looked-after children consistently perform far worse than children from similar socio-economic backgrounds who are not in local authority care. This is well-known to practitioners, as are many of the reasons why educational failure is so common. However, given the problem focused nature of much childcare practice, we know a lot more about why children fail, and tend to encounter far more children who fail than succeed. However, some looked-after children seem to do much better than others – is there anything we can learn from these 'survivors'?

Surviving the care system: education and resilience [4]

Moves in care, lack of staff continuity, absence of private space in which to do homework, and more generally, an environment in which education as a route to positive adult outcomes is undervalued are typical barriers to educational success that looked-after children encounter. Despite a variety of initiatives, the outcomes for children in care, compared to children in the general population, remain poor. This study located a group of 'high achievers' (n = 38) and matched them with a group of young people who had done less well. The pre-care circumstances of the two groups were similar, as were many dimensions of their in-care experiences. However, educationally successful children usually had a special relationship with at least one person who was able to offer them support and advice, few had significant periods of time outside school, most had learned to, and were supported in, learning to read early and had peer groups who were positive about the value of education.

The study concluded that support for looked after children's educational careers remains a far lower priority compared to other perceived needs in both residential and foster care settings, despite the well-attested benefits of investment in children's education. Replicating the factors associated with 'successful' children, along with other reforms, are essential strategies in attacking the educational failures of looked-after children.

Case study 2: Employment

People affected by psychological disorders suffer serious disadvantages in the job market. Failure to access open employment heightens the risk of poverty, social exclusion, low self-esteem and vulnerability to illness. There are various routes to open employment for people who may need extra help or support. Two common strategies are to prepare people for work in sheltered settings, and then place them in the open job market. Another is to find places in open employment, and provide support until the person is able to function independently. Which approach is more likely to lead to secure long term employment?

Helping people with severe mental illness obtain work: a systematic review [5]

This review compared outcomes – defined as success in finding competitive employment – from pre-vocational training and supported employment. Eleven trials met the review inclusion criteria. Subjects in supported employment were more likely than those in pre-vocational training to be in competitive employment at 18 months (31% v. 12%). Subjects in supported employment earned more and worked more hours per week than those who had received pre-vocational training. The review suggests that placing people directly in a work setting and supporting them is more likely to result in long term employment than a setting that provides training only with the intention of 'moving on' at a later date.

This study is also a good illustration of how research evidence can be of direct benefit to service users or their families in helping them to reach informed decisions about programme options. Where the knowledge base of practitioners includes a good understanding of relevant research, we are in a far better position to fully brief our clients on the respective merits of different approaches.

Case study 3: Reducing offending (1)

Some programmes which aim to divert young people from future offending behaviour have a more robust evidence base than others. For example, there is a strong body of evidence that suggests aggressive, military style 'boot camps' are ineffective, and are likely to increase, rather than decrease delinquency [6]. However, other programmes, which seek to increase young people's self-esteem and interpersonal skills through challenging group activities, show distinct promise.

Wilderness challenge programmes for delinquent youth: a meta-analysis [7]

The authors examined all studies of programmes which (a) involved delinquent youth aged 10–21 years in a 'wilderness' challenge and (b) featured a control group. In these programmes, young people typically participate in physically and mentally challenging activities, like back-packing or rock climbing. The theoretical basis of the programme is based on a belief that mastery of tasks will lead to greater self-esteem, a stronger locus of control, and an improved ability to work co-operatively. Twenty eight studies were identified. When the results of all these studies were combined, there was a clear benefit to the young people involved in the programmes, compared to those who were not, with particular improvements in self-esteem, pro-social behaviour and school adjustment. The most effective programmes were of high intensity, especially the physical activities, but also of short duration, and had more therapeutic enhancements.

Using the critical skills we have discussed in previous chapters, we might ask a number of questions as to whether this review – of American programmes – can be generalised to UK conditions. Programmes, even those of shorter duration, may last several weeks, an easier prospect in a country with rather more extensive wilderness areas than the UK. The programmes reviewed concerned a large majority of males, not females, and the physically demanding nature of the activities would not be appropriate or possible for some young people, especially those with physical impairments. However – while being careful not to draw precise parallels with schemes which may differ in some crucial aspects – a number of programmes with similar features, both in the UK and in other countries [8,9], have also been positively reviewed, suggesting that such approaches are worthy of consideration.[1]

Reducing offending (2)

As well as directing us towards interventions which enjoy support, we may also be warned that some popular interventions carry less evidential weight than may widely be supposed.

---

[1] More information about wilderness programmes and their effectiveness can be accessed at *www.wilderdom.com*

'Scared straight' and other juvenile awareness programmes for preventing juvenile delinquency [10]

These programmes are based on the premise that arranging organised visits to prisons for young offenders or young people at risk of offending may deter them from crime after witnessing prison life at first hand, and interacting with adult inmates. Programmes like these have operated world wide, including in the UK, and remain popular, with claims routinely made of significant success. Nine trials that randomly or quasi-randomly assigned young people to these programmes were identified. Eligible studies had to have a 'no-exposure' control and at least one outcome measure of 'post-visit' criminal behaviour. When the results were combined, the analysis pointed to a clear conclusion – the programmes were more harmful, in terms of their impact on offending rates, than doing nothing at all.

We have previously made the point that all interventions have the potential to cause harm as well as do good. Clearly, on the basis of this review, we would have strong evidential support for guiding a young person away from any involvement in such programmes; indeed, it is from examples like this that the strong symmetry between effectiveness and ethical behaviour in social care practice becomes most evident.

Reducing offending (3)

As we have illustrated in the examples above, in some cases the weight of evidence indicates a clear gain, in others a clear loss. In yet other cases, the jury remains out. For example, mentoring programmes have a long history in child welfare, especially programmes aimed at youths at risk of offending behaviour, which were being used in the UK by the Home Office well before World War Two. They are often very popular with both mentors and young people, and frequently attract praise and support from all parties, not least because their basic premise is very plausible. Programmes regularly receive high level backing, and make substantial claims, which stretch far beyond any impact on an individual child:

Research shows that adolescents who have an adult mentor are far less likely to engage in high-risk behaviours. Mentoring relationships . . . not only provide positive influences for individual children, but also strengthen families and communities.

(President George W. Bush, January 2004)

We know that children who become involved in anti-social peer group activities during the pre-adolescent period are at an elevated risk of becoming serial offenders as teenagers. Is it possible to divert young people from crime and anti-social behaviour by the recruitment of mentors in the middle school years?

One-to-one, non-directive mentoring programmes to reduce offending or other anti-social activities in young people [11]
This review examined mentoring programmes which support children who are exposed, because of their circumstances, to an enhanced risk of becoming involved in criminal activities. Literature from the UK and USA was examined, including both individual studies and meta-analyses. There was no consistent evidence found that young people with mentors were advantaged over those without, in terms of behaviour, school attendance and performance, offending rates or drug use. One well known study which had found a positive relationship was judged to be flawed because many young people most likely to 'fail' had been filtered out. Where benefits occurred, such as an overall fall in offending behaviour, it did not appear to be due to the mentoring itself. On the other hand, very positive accounts were routinely recorded by both young people and mentors themselves, many relationships persisted, and there was no clear evidence of harm. Drop outs from, or failure to recruit to mentoring schemes have a very substantial impact on cost, with the unit cost of one scheme in London increasing from £3,700 to £5,800, and another from £3,000 to £10,000 because of lower than anticipated attendance.

This example illustrates a number of important elements of evidence-based practice. First, that we must be able to cope with uncertainty, build on what we already know, and amend our knowledge base accordingly. Second, just because 'everyone knows something to be true', it does not necessarily mean that it is. Third, we must recognise that interventions that may be effective for one group of people, or in one situation, may not work in another and vice versa. Mentoring for example, may achieve highly desirable impacts on some aspects of social welfare, and fewer or none on others. Fourth, when we have a particularly strong investment in a certain approach, we tend to be reluctant to acknowledge that it may be less effective than we have claimed or, conversely, acknowledge that an approach we believed to be highly *in*effective actually works. Last, we must beware of final verdicts. Interventions which appear unsuccessful may achieve positive effects if a different approach is taken, by for example, varying the length, type or intensity of the work, recruiting more skilled staff, targeting a different population and so on.

Neat solutions to practice problems are, as we have acknowledged, and every practitioner knows, rarely available. Extensive dialogue within staff groups, focused on a specific practice problem may be required. Effective implementation processes begin with the agenda being agreed with those who have to do the implementing. This raises a typical problem. Questions that researchers like answering are rarely those that practitioners ask; similarly, researchers are not always good at dealing with the questions that practitioners actually want answered. The result is invariably a compromise, and the ensuing 'messiness' is, we would argue, inseparable from the process. For example, Figure 6.1 summarises an implementation procedure- designed as a poster presentation for the purposes of knowledge dissemination. It illustrates the process agreed between one of the authors and a group of practitioners who were keen to improve outcomes for children and young mothers where early attachment was proving problematic.

While in some situations, identifying a discrete, answerable practice question, reviewing the relevant literature, and recommending an evidence-based response that lies within the resource and skill base of the staff group is both possible and practical, this is not always the case. In this example, the process involved a variety of activities, not all of which were anticipated at the outset. This, and the other examples given show how, by paying attention to the evidence base, we can:

- Learn from people who have overcome adversities, and try to replicate these factors in a wider population.
- Be more certain that investing time and effort in a particular approach will result in the outcomes that we and service users want.
- Be able to choose between two or more approaches, each of which is trying to achieve the same outcome.
- Avoid investing in approaches that make no apparent contribution to the outcomes we are pursuing.
- Expose ourselves and our beliefs to reasonable scrutiny, have their worth confirmed, amend them, seek further assurance, or discard them as appropriate.

Obstacles to evidence-based practice

Despite the growing support and enthusiasm for the idea of evidence-based practice amongst social care professionals [12–14], a variety of obstacles can obstruct its realisation on a day to day basis. It is important to recognise these impediments to change in order to develop organisations which can

Getting Research into Practice- a pilot project
Tony Newman and Benny McDaniel

1. Context
PACT (Parent and Child Together) is a residential project that offers assessment and support to young women aged 16-24 years and their children from birth to three years. Young mothers are referred by social services throughout Northern Ireland. PACT aims to enable the parent and child to remain together where appropriate. When this is not possible PACT works with parents and professionals to make decisions about the children's futures.

2. Evidence Based Practice
This means that decisions made about the welfare of vulnerable people will be informed by critically appraised research evidence. PACT, like other Barnardo's services, wish to assure themselves, their funding bodies and their service users that services are based on robust evidence of effectiveness

3. Practitioners will use research if .....
➢ It is **very** accessible
➢ They can understand it
➢ It answers their practice questions
➢ They are supported and encouraged
➢ They believe it will benefit service users
➢ It enhances their professional status
➢ They are rewarded for doing so

4. The Process

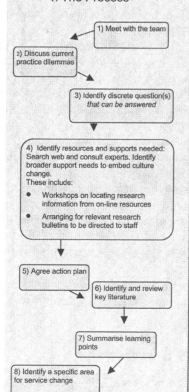

1) Meet with the team

2) Discuss current practice dilemmas

3) Identify discrete question(s) *that can be answered*

4) Identify resources and supports needed: Search web and consult experts. Identify broader support needs to embed culture change.
These include:
- Workshops on locating research information from on-line resources
- Arranging for relevant research bulletins to be directed to staff

5) Agree action plan

6) Identify and review key literature

7) Summarise learning points

8) Identify a specific area for service change

5. Outcomes

Research Question
What works in establishing attachment between mothers and infants in situations where the normal attachment processes have been interrupted or damaged?'

Key Learning Points
➢ Neglect impacts on attachment and needs to be addressed before intervention is likely to be effective
➢ Post natal depression impacts on attachment, however intervention can be successful, even when depression is present
➢ Short term interventions can be effective in improving attachment
➢ Video feedback with a supportive worker can be effective
➢ Interaction coaching, increasing social supports and alleviating maternal stress can help attachment

Key Areas for Service Change
➢ Video work to be integrated into the PACT assessment with all families. Key staff to be trained in using observation procedures.
➢ Parent-child interaction to be assessed in all families using existing measures, with additional measures of sensitivity
➢Closer attention to be paid to external stresses and developing social supports

Figure 6.1 Getting research into practice: a pilot project

effectively adopt evidence-based practices and policies. The main obstacles could be described as cultural, practical and structural.

The social care sector is often criticised as having an overly risk-averse culture, which can stifle the readiness of staff to break with tradition and try out new approaches, even when they have been shown to be effective. Social care has also been characterised as having a culture of action over reflection. For instance, many staff express the view that reading is not valued in their workplace, feeling that they have to be seen to be 'doing something' and that reading a journal article at their desk, or browsing the Internet for research, are simply not perceived as 'real work'. A further cultural obstacle is what has been described as 'new managerialism' in social care, a legacy of 1980s reforms which promoted cost-cutting, target chasing and the standardisation of services. While these reforms have had many positive outcomes, some social care staff regard excessive emphasis on performance indicators and targets as being detrimental to the use of research within practice, since the emphasis on monitoring and attainment of targets leaves little space for reflective analytical processes.

The impediments to evidence-based practice highlighted in the biggest available survey to date [15], which explored the views and knowledge of professional grade social care staff about evidence-based practice, were predominantly *practical* in nature. For instance, the main obstacles to keeping abreast of the professional literature identified, in order of importance, were a lack of time, the cost of books and journals, and poor access to the literature. Another important obstacle was lack of departmental support for reading research. Any reading which does take place occurs in practitioners' own time – a reflection of the fact that little or no time is allocated within working hours to such activity. Only 10 per cent of respondents in this survey reported having any protected time for reading or professional development.

When asked what methods could be used by departments to encourage the practical use of research findings, respondents rated as most important increased availability of technical research facilities such as databases and the internet, protected study time, and opportunities to attend research meetings. Other research supports the argument that lack of time, and poor access to relevant literature, are key hurdles to evidence-based practice. [16]

Structural obstacles relate to features of the social care workforce, its training and education system, and the way in which research is produced, commissioned and rewarded. The survey referred to above highlighted a deficit in critical appraisal skills and a lack of familiarity with research literature, problems which are arguably a result of the absence of research training on social work qualification courses [17]. Workforce issues include staffing shortages (currently a national problem), which result in extremely heavy workloads for existing staff, leaving them with little time for keeping up to date with research developments. There is also a need for those who produce, commission and fund research, to communicate their findings in a way which meets the needs of practitioners, policy makers and managers [18]. For instance, research should be accessible, timely and relevant. Currently there is little incentive for universities to disseminate their research findings more widely to practitioner and policy audiences, because performance is assessed largely by the number of publications in so-called 'high impact' journals (to which few staff in non-university settings have easy access).

Acknowledging that there are practical, cultural and structural obstacles, what can we actually do to help incorporate evidence into everyday practice? Although there are institutional hurdles which need to be addressed, requiring efforts from senior managers as well as policy makers, there are nevertheless many practical measures that frontline staff and organisations can and do take to encourage ongoing organisational learning and use of evidence.

Improving opportunities to access and read research

Establish a research newsletter, forum, or e-mail list

In-house evidence-related newsletters are one way of increasing access to research within an organisation. These would essentially be updates of new research, distributed to both practitioners and managers. The format, style and content of such newsletters are important. Existing research suggests that the impact of these publications will be greater when information is presented in summary form, using jargon-free language, with practice implications drawn out. Newsletters may be provided through a variety of media, including e-mail bulletins, your organisational intranet, in-trays and staff notice boards. It may also be worth setting up an online forum or e-mail list. Such a facility would be useful for staff wanting to keep up to date with internal research activity, including any local evaluations or research projects underway. Some organisations maintain their own in-house databases of locally conducted research or 'grey' (i.e. unpublished) literature. A good example of this is being developed by Wiltshire County Council.

Example: Wiltshire County Council Pathways Service

The Wiltshire Pathways project (*www.wiltshirepathways.org*) is part of the county's multi-agency children and young people's partnership. Their website contains a wide range of information for professionals working with children within the county. Part of the Pathways project is concerned with ensuring that children with mental health problems are directed swiftly and efficiently to the service that can best meet their needs. In order to help professionals stay fully informed about effective treatment, a section of the website – which can only be accessed by password – provides details of effective interventions within common categories of childhood problems, such as self-injury, poor school attendance, attention disorders, or substance misuse. Within each category, current best evidence is summarised in relation to children of different ages. By consulting the relevant section, professionals can fully inform themselves about the specific issue, provide the intervention themselves if they are adequately trained, or refer the young person to an appropriate specialist. At the time of writing, this site was under development and will be fully operational in 2005.

Build up your library resources

Establishing or improving internal library resources is an essential step in increasing access to research. We have already highlighted the wealth of information available through journals, the internet, databases, libraries and so on. Organisations might wish to purchase subscriptions to a few key research journals in social work and related fields so that practitioners have readily available research to hand. To ensure staff are able to find out what other published research is out there, it is also essential that they have access to research databases. While your starting point would be to use freely available databases, your organisation may also wish to subscribe to other specialist databases such as ChildData, or ASSIA (see Chapter 7 for more details) so that staff do not miss out on important research not indexed on the free databases.

Example: Dorset County Council Social Services

Dorset Social Services has made accessing research easier for its practitioners by subscribing to five online social work journals, and the Social Care and Health Library (containing 4,000 items). It also produces its own Good Practice Research Series, which provides practical advice on topics such as research ethics, questionnaire design, and locating research.

Individual teams may wish to establish resource areas within their offices, with dedicated book cases or filing cabinets for housing articles and reports, and posters highlighting the research support available within the organisation. Different individuals in a team could take responsibility for collecting research on their own specialist area of interest, and placing this information in the resource area for colleagues to share. This should save both time and money, by avoiding duplicate purchases of the same publications.

It is well worth establishing a good relationship with your local university and college libraries, especially those with departments of social work. They will often be willing to allow access to their facilities, sometimes including borrowing rights for staff working in social services departments where their students are placed. Librarians can be enormously helpful in advising on locating research and conducting literature searches. Students on placement can be a useful resource in themselves, since they are able to access university or college library facilities, including databases and journals. Your department may also wish to advertise information about how to use your local library's inter-library loans service, so that staff know how to get hold of photocopied journal articles.

Set aside some protected reading time

It is one thing to be able to access research and quite another to find time in a busy schedule to read it. As discussed above, time for reading is a precious commodity and this presents a major obstacle to promoting evidence-based social care. However, a revised post-qualifying framework for the social care workforce, which places an emphasis on evidence-based practice [19], and the establishment of the new social work degree course and social care register [20], are positive indicators of a maturing profession that recognises the need for staff who are well qualified both in practice and research terms. Some social workers, to whom the authors have spoken, feel it is their own personal responsibility to find time for reading; others feel employers should build protected time for this into workload planning. With staff shortages in many departments, heavy caseloads, and increasingly complex cases, this can be difficult. However, as we have argued throughout, being up to date with research is essential both on professional and ethical grounds. Clearly, time has to be found within the working week to read and reflect on research, practice and policy. Some practitioners, for example, set aside half an hour at the beginning of each day to browse the latest journal issue in their field. Research evidence from the public health field indicates that people are more likely to take regular exercise if it fits into their daily routine [21]. In a similar way, research may be more widely read by social care and health professionals if opportunities to do so can be slotted into existing day to day working practices.

Creating opportunities to discuss research

Discuss research at meetings

We need to have the chance not merely to read research but to discuss it with peers, and to reflect on what it might mean for practice. Team or departmental meetings can present the ideal opportunity for such discussion and debate. Some departments regularly invite researchers along to their meetings to present their work, allowing staff to ask questions and seek clarification. Staff are then given the opportunity to discuss the implications with those responsible for conducting the study. This is of benefit not only to practitioners but for researchers, since it provides them with feedback about how their research is received and made use of within a practice setting, and raises awareness amongst academics about the needs of the professionals for whom they are writing. Departments might wish to consider having a series of seminars on different research issues, inviting speakers from local universities to present on a range of social care topics. Practitioners could also be invited to present their own in-house research or service evaluations.

Example: South Gloucestershire

South Gloucestershire recently held a series of seminars and workshops to which all evidence-based 'reps.' were invited. In the seminars, researchers presented up to date research in their specialist field.

The following seminar topics were discussed:

- Promoting resilience in families: a review of research on effective strategies for childcare services;
- Effectiveness and cost effectiveness research on intermediate care services for older people on discharge from hospital.

Workshops were held on the following themes:

- Critical appraisal skills for social workers: judging the quality and relevance of research;
- How to evaluate your service;
- How to locate social care research on the internet.

Discuss research in supervision

Discussions about research can be built into supervision meetings. For example, through your literature searching, you may encounter studies that describe a more effective approach to a particular social problem relevant to your work. However, you are not trained to provide that method. Your supervisor may be able to help you address this problem, either by finding a suitable programme of training, or by locating a specialist to whom you could refer your clients. Supervision can provide the time and space needed to work through the process of applying research to individual cases. As stated in the National Occupational Standards for Social Work [22], staff must 'critically reflect upon (their) own practice and performance using supervision and support systems'. Part of critical reflection on practice, we would argue, involves assessing the extent to which the approaches used are evidence-based. We recognise that there are obstacles to this, for example supervision is often taken up with dealing with crises, monitoring and risk assessments. Indeed the aforementioned CEBSS survey found that in 1998, 60 per cent of social care staff reported that they rarely or never discussed research in supervision meetings. Therefore, despite the potential benefits of using supervision for this purpose, the current realities of practice mean it can be difficult to achieve. For this reason, you may wish to ensure that research is included as one of the criteria on the checklists or monitoring forms you use for individual clients within supervision.

Start or join a journal club

Journal clubs are an increasingly popular way of ensuring that practitioners get the opportunity to discuss research with colleagues on a regular basis. The idea of a journal club is to meet at regular intervals to discuss an individual research study or review. Groups often meet over lunch provided by the department. Prior to each meeting, a research paper is distributed to everyone in the group. Each person reads the article and comes prepared to discuss it. A different person takes responsibility for choosing and distributing the research paper each time, to ensure the workload is spread evenly. Whilst journal clubs seem to generate enthusiasm and increase awareness about research, it is important that they do not run out of steam. The suggestions that follow may help maintain momentum and get the most out of your journal club.

Example: Devon Occupational Therapists

A group of occupational therapists at a recent critical appraisal skills course run by CEBSS commented that although they found their journal club useful, they felt their discussions lacked structure. They believed it would help not simply to read and discuss the implications of the research, but critically to evaluate its strengths and weaknesses. They decided that a solution would be to use the critical appraisal 'tools' or instruments developed by CEBSS (see Chapter 3), to work through individual pieces of research. The group felt that attending a course on critical appraisal skills training was a worthwhile activity for anyone involved in a journal club. Other suggestions included offering lunch as an enticement, and rewarding attendance with credits towards Continuing Professional Development (CPD) requirements.

Example: Plymouth Occupational Therapists

In a Plymouth based journal club members present papers in groups rather than individually. This makes the presentations more varied and increases participation and discussion. Those involved try to ensure that the research does not stay within the confines of the group: there is an active commitment to communicate key findings to other staff. In addition, topics for discussion are set to reflect departmental priorities. This is done by sending questionnaires to practice supervisors and practitioners in which they are asked to identify practice areas for which they would like to locate research.

Creating and sustaining an evidence-based culture

Create an evidence-based strategy

There are a number of additional activities or initiatives that can be undertaken to promote an evidence-based culture, and *evidence-based strategies* provide a good overall framework for this. Strategies that have already been developed by social services departments in the south west of England provide some good examples. For instance, some make a commitment to acquiring subscriptions to three or four key social care research journals. Others attempt to strengthen links with local academic institutions to ensure that the expertise and resources available in these institutions are fully exploited. Some strategies focus on improving the communication of research findings, for example through newsletters or internal e-mail bulletins. They also schedule annual workshops or conferences that promote the use of research within practice, and include a commitment to ensuring that all staff training is, as far as possible, evidence-based. Some build research activity into Continuing Professional Development programmes and Post Qualifying

Awards with training in skills for evidence-based practice being a compulsory part of post qualifying training in certain local authorities. The Centre for Evidence-Based Social Services and the What Works for Children? project have jointly produced an evidence guide which can help in this regard [23]. It outlines a step-by-step approach to evidence-based social care and comprises of six individual modules which can be used as a self-directed learning resource or as a training resource. The modules come with slides and activities that can be used in training sessions.

Your organisation may wish to create a list of practice related research topics it feels need to be investigated, which could be sent to local universities to be undertaken by PhD or Masters students. It may also be helpful to agree on some overarching thematic priorities for studies by external, professional researchers, to ensure that research is led by the priorities of the organisation.

Departments that do not already employ research or information staff to support evidence-based practice could consider establishing one or two such posts. In our experience, organisations with such posts tend to be further forward in terms of evidence-based practice. Typically, these staff members help practitioners and managers to locate research, advise them on evaluation methodology, and provide training in locating, understanding and applying research. Additionally, they often undertake to circulate relevant research throughout the organisation, for example via newsletters, as discussed above. If resources do not permit such posts, research skills or awareness could be tied into some job descriptions and recruitment criteria.

By creating an evidence-based strategy, organisations become accountable for achieving the goals and principles set out within it. Where possible, a strategy should be backed by a steering group, with members from all levels of the organisation represented. Team action plans, with key action points, can help with the implementation of aims and objectives set out in the overall strategy, and assist in maintaining momentum for evidence-based practice. Teams could devise these plans individually to suit their own needs and capacities.

Audit your organisation's research mindedness

Organisations striving to increase research use may wish to consider using an appropriate self-assessment tool to evaluate the current state of play and to identify areas where improvements are needed. One tool, developed by the Canadian Health Services Research Foundation in Ontario, has been adapted by the Evidence Network's 'What Works for Children?' project and is available online.[2] In addition, Research in Practice (RIP) has created the 'REAL audit tool'

---

[2] *http://www.whatworksforchildren.org.uk/docs/tools/SelfAssessmtWEB.pdf*

and the 'REAL team action pack toolkit'.[3] The first of these allows you to establish baseline information about how evidence-based your organisation is, and the second provides a practical framework for building capacity. Those wishing to assess their 'research mindedness' should look at the Research Mindedness Virtual Learning Resource. This contains a 'practitioner entry point', with an online self-assessment tool, and is an excellent overall introduction to the main steps of evidence-based practice.[4]

Join an evidence-based group, become an evidence-based champion

A number of social services departments have their own evidence-based groups. Members of these groups act as evidence-based 'reps.', attending any research events being held locally and sharing information or materials obtained with colleagues in their own teams. These reps, sometimes known as evidence-based 'champions', are often practitioners who have carried out some research of their own, and who can enthuse others to do likewise by showing them that it can be done, and providing advice where needed.

Example: Dave Pitcher

A real life example is Dave Pitcher, who is a social worker in Plymouth, Devon. When a couple who wanted to foster their grandchild approached his department, Dave was asked to conduct an assessment of the couple. They challenged Dave about what right he had to see whether or not they were competent to care for members of their own family. This challenge led him to reflect on the issues faced by grandparents who care. He conducted a literature search and discovered that there was very little research exploring the needs and experiences of this group, and so, he decided to conduct his own research project. The research involved interviews with 33 sets of grandparent carers. This not only provided him with information to help his own practice, but also started to fill a gap in the research base. Dave has presented the results of his research at a number of conferences and events, and has had his research published [24] and indexed on the CareData database (see Chapter 2). His findings have led to improved services for grandparent carers in the area, including the establishment of a support group and a telephone listening service.

---

[3] *http://www.rip.org.uk/changeprojects/org_support.htm*
[4] *http://www.resmind.swap.ac.uk/index.htm*

Evaluate your service

There are a number of reasons why conducting service evaluations may help create and sustain an evidence-based culture. Firstly, it has been shown in a number of studies that practitioners who have been involved in carrying out research are generally more inclined to use research to guide their practice [25]. Secondly, being familiar with the research process and its potential pitfalls means one is more likely to maintain a critical eye when reading other people's research. Finally, the relevance of a study is an important factor determining its uptake by practitioners; locally conducted research is more likely to be perceived as being relevant to practice. For detailed and practical information on conducting service evaluations, readers are advised to consult one of the many resources available on this subject [26–28].

If you are considering an evaluation, a few words of caution are necessary. One of the main difficulties with in-house evaluation is that time and resource constraints often dictate that we settle for small-scale studies, using basic (and sometimes downright flawed) research designs. As already discussed in this book, not all evidence is of equal value. Equally, limited evidence is not always better than no evidence, if it is of poor quality. For this reason it is essential that if you are conducting an evaluation, you are clear about any methodological limitations or shortcomings of the investigation, and do not give undue weight to its findings. Before considering an evaluation, it is important to check the literature to see if existing research already answers your research question, thus preventing the reinvention of wheels.

Before undertaking an evaluation, be aware of the practical and logistical demands of such an exercise. For instance, under the incoming Research Governance Framework in social care [29], all research (rather than audit) being conducted in social services departments in England will have to pass through what are known as 'research ethics committees' and 'scientific review panels'. These bodies assess the quality and ethics of the proposed research before allowing it to proceed.

It is also essential that realistic costings are calculated and a timetable agreed, with the necessary resources allocated for the research to be completed and disseminated successfully. It is worth consulting an experienced researcher for advice on this matter, and including them on your evaluation steering group. The more complicated aspects of the research, particularly data collection and analysis, may well require input from a trained researcher. In sum, it is worth considering the opportunity costs of an evaluation. Given the time, resources and commitment required to conduct an evaluation, will the results be worth it? Will the study be of a rigorous enough design to use it to guide or inform service development? Or is there already research out there which answers your question? This should always be the starting point before embarking on an evaluation.

Communicate effectively

Organisations that engage in some or all of the activities described in this chapter must, of course, ensure that staff are aware of what is going on. We have been surprised at the number of practitioners we encounter who are unaware of the research related support services available and activities underway within their organisations. This may be down to the difficulties of communicating effectively in a complex organisation, or to high staff turnover, or it may simply be due to heavy workloads. One way to improve communication is to ensure that all new staff are fully informed about the research resources, events and support available to them as part of their induction process. Colourful posters and flyers could be put up on the walls of training departments, area offices or in common rooms, to highlight the research activities taking place and resources available. Internal e-mail distribution lists or newsletters can also be effective in generating awareness.

If you are involved in disseminating research findings within your organisation, you may wish to consider using a range of outlets and approaches, since more traditional, passive methods, such as one off in-service training sessions or lectures, have been shown to have little impact by themselves [30]. Active forms of dissemination, which tailor the format and style of oral or written materials to suit different audiences, and provide the opportunity for discussion, may be more effective. Colleagues, role models and opinion leaders have been shown to be influential in encouraging uptake of research findings. Interventions which involve providing clients with research-based information have also been shown to have a good impact. In addition, there is evidence to support collaborative approaches to research dissemination. Where practitioners and academics are co-located or are linked in some form of partnership, research is more likely to be used by staff. Key features present in organisations which are most likely to succeed in getting evidence into practice are as follows:

Organisational features that can aid research utilisation
- A corporate culture that rewards flexibility, innovation, change and continuous improvement (change is not always what is needed, but an organisation must be *willing* to do so for research findings to influence practice).
- Good systems in place to ensure research findings are fed back into practice and policy.
- Effective communication channels.
- Opportunities to discuss and debate research and practice.

- Flexibility in resource allocation and programme management to ensure changes can be put into place as new research comes to light.
- Tying local performance indicators to research.
- Encouragement of local evaluations, as long as they are sound enough methodologically to be used to inform practice.
- A culture that values reading, research and reflection.
- A culture that is not overly risk-averse.
- Joint working, which can lead to a 'cross fertilisation' of ideas.
- Acknowledgement that evidence-based practice takes time and resources and that staff shortages and over-heavy workloads militate against its realisation.

Conclusion

Research rarely mirrors the exact characteristics, experiences and circumstances of service users, and it may be difficult to locate individual studies which directly answer all of our practice questions. However, good research does provide broad messages about the effectiveness of different approaches to social care with various client groups, and information about people's views and needs. Once this information has been located (and its trustworthiness appraised) the practitioner can then make a judgement about its relevance and applicability to the case in hand, and in combination with the preferences of the individual client, proceed to make an informed, and where appropriate mutually agreed, decision about the best course of action.

However, in order to arrive at this position the practitioner needs to have ready access to the research base, the skills to appraise its findings and the time to read and digest it, all – according to the available evidence – scarce commodities in the social care sector. What has become clear to those of us working to improve the relationship between research and practice is that there is little necessary relationship between research production, research dissemination and actual *implementation*. The latter is labour intensive, easily diverted by more acute priorities, dependent on small numbers of champions and subject to drift and diversion. Implementation programmes are also, despite being the most important part of the research into practice process, the least resourced, the least prestigious and the least rewarded. Nonetheless, an infinite number of excuses can be found to delay any implementation process – lack of time, lack of resources, a need for yet more research, missing stakeholder groups, concerns about sustainability – but as in any other process, learning occurs through doing. The activities and initiatives outlined in this chapter, and the approaches discussed in this book, indicate that although cultural, structural and practical obstacles remain to be addressed, there are nonetheless many ways in which practitioners and frontline managers can take action to increase the research-mindedness of themselves and their organisations. This, however, can only be achieved effectively if researchers and practitioners learn more about each other's trades, and together focus on building knowledge of the core source of 'evidence' – the experience, needs and aspirations of service users.

References

[1] Voltaire (1999) *Candide, or Optimism*. Hertfordshire: Wordsworth.

[2] Bero, L.A., Grilli, R., Grimshaw, J.M., Harvey, E., Oxman, A.D. and Thomson, M.A. (1998) Closing the gap between research and practice: an overview of systematic reviews of interventions to promote the implementation of research findings. *British Medical Journal*, 317, 465-68.

[3] Walter, I., Nutley, S. and Davies, H. (2003) *Research Impact: A Cross Sector Literature Review*. Research Unit for Research Utilisation, University of St. Andrews.

[4] Jackson, S. and Martin, P. (1998) Surviving the care system: education and resilience. *Journal of Adolescence*. 21: 569-83.

[5] Crowther, R., Marshall, M., Bond, G. and Huxley, P. (2001) Helping people with severe mental illness find work: systematic review. *British Medical Journal*. 322: 204-8.

[6] Utting, D. and Vennard, J. (2000) *What Works With Young Offenders in the Community?* Ilford: Barnardo's.

[7] Wilson, S.J. and Lipsey, M.W. (1999) Wilderness challenge programmes for delinquent youth: a meta-analysis of outcome evaluations. *Evaluation and Programme Planning*. 23, 1-12. Available at: *www.vanderbilt.edu/CERM*.

[8] Wrangham, J. and Crowley, J. (2001) Partnership for youth. *Youth Crime Wales*. 3: Winter, 8-9.

[9] Neill, J.T. and Dias, K.L. (2001) Adventure education and resilience: the double-edged sword. *Journal of Adventure Education and Outdoor Learning*. 1: 2, 35-42

[10] Petrosino, A., Turpin-Petrosino, C. and Buehler, J. (2002) *'Scared Straight' and Other Juvenile Awareness Programmes for Preventing Juvenile Delinquency*. Campbell Database of Systematic Reviews. Issue 4. Available at: *www.campbellcollaboration.org/doc-pdf/ssr.pdf*

[11] Lucas, P. and Liabo, K. (2002) One-to-one, non-directive mentoring programmes have not been shown to improve behaviour in young people involved in offending or anti-social activities. *What Works for Children Group Evidence Nugget*. April. Available at: *www.what-worksforchildren.org.uk*.

[12] Sheldon, B. and Chilvers, R. (2000) *Evidence-Based Social Care: A Study of Prospects and Problems*. Lyme Regis: Russell House Publishing.

[13] Booth, S.H., Booth, A. and Falzon, L.J. (2003) The need for information and research skills training to support evidence-based social care: a literature review and survey. *Learning in Health and Social Care*. 2: 4, 191-201.

[14] Walter, I., Nutley, S., Percy-Smith, J., McNeish, D. and Frost, S. (2004) *Improving the Use of Research in Social Care Practice*. Knowledge Review 7. London: Social Care Institute for Excellence.

[15] Sheldon, B., Chilvers, R., Ellis, A., Moseley, A. and Tierney, S. (in press) A pre-post empirical study of obstacles to, and opportunities for, evidence-based practice in social care. In Bilson, A. (Ed.) *Evidence-Based Practice and Social Work: International Research and Policy Perspectives*. London: Whiting and Birch.

[16] Hughes, M., McNeish, D., Newman, T., Roberts, H. and Sachdev, D. (2000) *What Works? Making Connections: Linking Research and Practice*. Ilford: Barnardo's/Joseph Rowntree Foundation.

[17] Sheldon, B. and Macdonald, G. (1999) *Research and Practice in Social Care: Mind the Gap.* Centre for Evidence-Based Social Services, University of Exeter.

[18] Barratt, M. (2003) Organizational support for evidence-based practice within child and family social work. *Child and Family Social Work.* 8: 143–150.

[19] General Social Care Council (GSCC). (2001) *Social Work Education Post-Qualifying Training Handbook.*

[20] *http://www.gscc.org.uk/*

[21] Hillsdon, M., Foster, C., Naidoo, B. and Crombie, H. (2004) *The Effectiveness of Public Health Interventions for Increasing Physical Activity Among Adults: A Review of Reviews.* London: Health Development Agency.

[22] TOPSS UK. (2002) *The National Occupational Standards for Social Work: Working Copy.*

[23] Frost, S., Moseley, A., Tierney, S., Hutton, A., Ellis, A., Duffy, M., and Newman, T. (forthcoming) *The Evidence Guide: Using Research and Evaluation in Social Care and Allied Professions.* Barkingside: Barnardo's/Centre for Evidence-Based Social Services.

[24] Pitcher, D. (2002) Going to live with grandma. *Professional Social Work.* June 2002 14-15.

[25] Walter, I., Nutley, S. and Davies, H. (2003) *Research Impact: A Cross Sector Literature Review.* Research Unit for Research Utilisation, University of St. Andrews.

[26] Shaw, I. and Lishman, J. (Eds.) (1999) *Evaluation and Social Work Practice.* London: Sage.

[27] Boruch, R.F. (1997) *Randomized Experiments for Planning and Evaluation: A Practical Guide.* Applied Social Research Methods Series, Vol. 44. London: Sage.

[28] Fitz-Gibbon, C.T. and Morris, L.L. (1987) *How to Design a Program Evaluation.* London: Sage.

[29] Nutley, S., Percy-Smith, J. and Solesbury, W. (2003) *Models of Research Impact: A Cross-Sector Review of Literature and Practice.* Learning and Skills Research Centre. *www.psda.org.uk/files/PDF/1418.pdf.*

[30] Department of Health (2001) Research Governance Framework for Health and Social Care. London: Department of Health.

Resources for Evidence-based Social Work

The following pages contain lists of key resources to aid you in evidence-based practice. These are ordered by chapter, to make it easy to dip in and out of relevant sections as you read through the book. There are short descriptions of the most important resources mentioned in the book as well as brief details of some additional ones that may be of interest.

Some web site addresses will change as time goes on. If you type in the web address given and have problems, we suggest using a search engine such as Google or Alta Vista to locate the material. Simply type the name of the resource into a search engine box, e.g. 'centre for evidence-based social services', and click 'search'. Alternatively, you may be redirected automatically to the new page.

For those new to the Internet, you may wish to consult one of the introductory online tutorials or printed guides to using the Internet mentioned under the resources list for Section 2 'Accessing research'.

Chapter 1: Introducing Evidence-Based Practice

Online materials

Campbell Collaboration   *www.campbellcollaboration.org*

Contains a database of trials (C2-SPECTR) and a database of systematic reviews (C2-RIPE) in education, social welfare and criminal justice.

Centre for Evidence-Based Social Services (CEBSS)   *www.cebss.org*

Contains advice on locating research and using research evidence, online tutorials for using the Internet, news about CEBSS' events, and access to all of the Centre's publications, including its newsletters.

Cochrane Collaboration   *www.cochrane.org/index0.htm*

Set up in 1993, the Cochrane Collaboration produces systematic and up-to-date reviews in healthcare (including reviews of psychosocial interventions).

Evidence-Based Medicine   *www.evidence-based-medicine.co.uk*

This electronic resource contains information about understanding evidence-based practice. The 'What is . . .' series of publications (which can be downloaded from this site) are particularly useful.

Introduction to Evidence-Based Occupational Therapy
                    www.cebm.utoronto.ca/syllabi/occ/intro.htm
A webpage that talks about evidence-based practice in relation to occupational therapy. It also contains a list of useful references.

Research in Practice (RIP)   *www.rip.org.uk*

RIP aims to promote the use of evidence to improve services for children and families. A range of useful resources can be found on this website, including access to publications by this organisation and other research resources.

Research Mindedness Virtual Learning Resource   *www.resmind.swap.ac.uk*

Funded by the Social Care Institute for Excellence (SCIE), the aim of this site is to help social care students and practitioners to use evidence to support their work.

Social Care Institute for Excellence (SCIE)   *www.scie.org.uk*

SCIE aims to promote good practice in social care, by reviewing knowledge to find out what works best for clients. This website has a range of useful links, including information about this organisation, access to its publications and a link to the Electronic Library for Social Care (eLSC).

Printed materials

Gibbs, L.E. (2003) *Evidence-Based Practice for the Helping Professions: A Practical Guide with Multimedia.* Pacific Grove, CA: Brooks/Cole.

This book provides an overview to evidence-based practice and also discusses how to practice in an evidence-based manner. It comes with a CD-ROM to allow for a 'hands-on' approach to learning.

Gomm, R. and Davies, C. (Eds.) (2000) *Using Evidence in Health and Social Care.* London: Sage Publications/Open University.

A collection of chapters, aimed at practitioners in health and social care, exploring different types of research design, and about using research in practice.

Law, M. and Baum, C. (1998) Evidence-based occupational therapy. *Canadian Journal of Occupational Therapy,* 65: 3, 131–5.

Provides background information about evidence-based practice in occupational therapy.

Sheldon, B. and Macdonald, G. (1999) *Research and Practice in Social Care: Mind The Gap.* Exeter: Centre for Evidence-Based Social Services.
An introduction to evidence-based practice in social care, providing arguments as to the importance of using research to inform professional decision-making.

Trinder, L. with Reynolds, S. (Eds.) (2000) *Evidence-Based Practice: A Critical Appraisal.* Oxford: Blackwell Science.
A general introduction to, and critical look at, the emergence of evidence-based practice in a range of professions, with chapters on social work and probation, health, education, public health and mental health.

Chapter 2: Accessing Research

Online materials

Accessing Social Care Research: An Introductory Guide
www.cebss.org/accessing_research.html
An online resource (also available in hard copy) that provides advice to practitioners about accessing social care research, from traditional material (such as books and journal articles) to online resources.

AgeInfo   *www.elsc.org.uk*
AgeInfo is an information service about old age and ageing. It provides a range of searchable databases. This resource is freely available via the Electronic Library for Social Care.

ASSIA (Applied Social Sciences Index and Abstracts)
www.csa.com/csa/factsheets/assia.shtml
A database including abstracts to articles from 650 international journals relevant to social services, psychology, sociology, education, health and other social science disciplines. The date range is 1987 to the present day. This database requires a subscription.

Barnardo's   *www.barnardos.org.uk*
From an evidence-based practice perspective, a useful section of this website is under 'Resources', entitled 'Research and publications'. Here, you can find summary (and some full) copies of reports, reviews and research carried out by Barnardo's on the theme of young people, children and their families.

Be-Evidence-Based   *www.be-evidence-based.com*

An electronic database of social care research owned and managed by the Centre for Evidence-Based Social Services (CEBSS), available free of charge through the CEBSS website or the Electronic Library for Social Care. It contains summaries of primary research articles, which are critically appraised with practice implications given. Also has a 'web tutorials' section to help those new to the Internet.

British Institute of Learning Disabilities   *www.bild.org.uk*

This website contains information about research carried out by this organisation and about publications produced by it.

British Medical Journal   *http://bmj.bmjjournals.com/*

You can download articles from this journal dating back to 1994. It contains a number of papers that would be relevant to social workers.

CareData   *www.elsc.org.uk/caredata/caredata.htm*

A freely available database of social care research, best practice guides, policy documents, and other information. Those using this resource can search via keywords, author, title of a document, or journal. An online help page is available.

Centre for Reviews and Dissemination (CRD)

www.york.ac.uk/inst/crd/darehp.htm

Contains references to systematic reviews and access to searchable databases. It is relevant to those involved in health and social care.

ChildData   *www.childdata.org.uk*

A database developed by the National Children's Bureau, which contains references to academic literature, but also to information on conferences, news items and key organisations. Requires a subscription.

Clinical Evidence   *www.nelh.nhs.uk/clinical_evidence.asp*

This website is provided via the National electronic Library for Health. It contains regularly updated evidence about the effectiveness of care.

Electronic Library for Social Care (eLSC)   *www.elsc.org.uk*

A free online resource owned and managed by the Social Care Institute for Excellence (SCIE). It aims to provide social care practitioners and managers with access to research and includes the database 'Caredata' (see above). This resource includes sections on 'Practice, Guidance and Standards', 'SCIE Best Practice Guidelines', 'Skills Building' and a 'Users and Carers' area. In addition, it has a 'Social Care Resources' section, with free access to the journals 'Research Policy and Planning' and 'Social Work in Europe'.

ERIC   *www.eric.ed.gov*

The Educational Resources Information Center (ERIC) is a freely available database produced in the USA which aims to increase access to education research and practice. It contains over 1,200,000 documents and journal articles on education research and practice written since 1966.

Evidence Network   *www.evidencenetwork.org*

A resource providing access to social science research publications relevant to policy and practice. Contains individual 'nodes' in a range of areas including social care related fields, which produce their own research publications, systematic reviews and discussion papers. These can be browsed by node or searched collectively. Provides an alphabetical and searchable index of key resources including databases, gateways and websites of research and evidence-based policy or practice centres.

Internet Social Worker   *www.vts.rdn.ac.uk/tutorial/social-worker*

A free online tutorial designed to improve information seeking skills on the Internet, specifically designed for social workers.

Joseph Rowntree Foundation   *www.jrf.org.uk/*

Contains research funded by this organisation into housing, social care and social policy.

Occupational therapy and disability websites
                            www2.plymouth.ac.uk/millbrook/links/linkhom.htm

A resource containing links to websites relevant to occupational therapists and others working with people with disabilities.

OT Direct   *www.otdirect.co.uk*

This is an independent site for occupational therapists (OTs), OT assistants and OT students. It contains links to useful websites relevant to practitioners in its 'Research' section.

OT Seeker   *www.otseeker.com/*

A database of abstracts (randomised controlled trials and systematic reviews), relevant to occupational therapists, which have been critically appraised.

PubMed   *www.pubmed.com*

A freely available database provided by the National Library of Medicine in the United States. It offers access to the internationally known MEDLINE, and one or two other medical databases. PubMed is of obvious importance to the medical social worker, but others may find its coverage touches on areas of interest. For example, those working in mental health, with older people, people with learning or physical disabilities, or in child protection may find it useful.

Regard   *www.regard.ac.uk/regard/home/index_html?*

Regard is an online database containing information on social science research funded by the Economic and Social Research Council (ESRC).

SCARE briefings   *www.elsc.org.uk/briefings/*

These online briefings provide summaries of information on particular topics to support joint working between health and social care.

Social Science Information Gateway (SOSIG)   *www.sosig.ac.uk*

A specialist gateway, which contains a selection of links to online resources that have been carefully chosen for their quality by subject specialists in the social sciences. It contains an area devoted to social welfare, which includes a section on social work.

The Centre for Policy on Ageing   *www.cpa.org.uk/index.html*

This website includes a publications section and a policy/research section, as well as access to databases such as AgeInfo (see above), and the NAIC database (National Aging Information Center), available free of charge. Also provides details of the Centre's Information Service and Reference Library, which is open to the public by appointment.

The Mental Health Foundation

www.mentalhealth.org.uk/

A number of full text documents are available at this website, which can be downloaded free of charge. Go to the 'Publications' section for further information.

The Norah Fry Research Centre   *www.bris.ac.uk/Depts/NorahFry*

As well as containing information about the Centre's current projects, this website includes a list of its publications, with a downloadable order form for ease of purchase.

The Royal College of Psychiatrists   *www.rcpsych.ac.uk/index.htm*

This site contains access to the 'College Research Unit' and a 'Publications' section, both of which may contain relevant information to practitioners working with clients who have a mental health problem.

What Works For Children? *www.whatworksforchildren.org.uk*

Under the 'Resources' part of this site there is a section called 'Evidence nuggets', which provides evidence on topics such as mentoring, parenting, cognitive-behavioural therapy, breakfast clubs, home visiting and traffic calming. Also on this site (again under 'Resources') is a section entitled 'Research briefings', which contains summaries of existing literature reviews in social care, offending and education. An excellent, user friendly resource for all working in the field of childcare.

Printed materials

Dawes, M., Davies, P., Gray, A., Mant, J., Seers, K. and Snowball, R. (2000) *Evidence-Based Practice: A Primer for Health Care Professionals.* London: Churchill Livingstone.

A book chapter outlining the main resources to search for information once you have formulated search questions. Covers key databases and websites in the Health Care field.

Gibbs, L.E. (2003). *Evidence-Based Practice for the Helping Professions: A Practical Guide with Multimedia.* Pacific Grove, CA: Brooks/Cole.

Contains a chapter about locating the best available evidence to answer your search question, including advice about devising a suitable search strategy.

Macwilliam, S., Maggs, P., Caldwell, A. and Tierney, S. (2003) *Accessing Social Care Research: An Introductory Guide.* Centre for Evidence-Based Social Services, University of Exeter.

A booklet that provides advice to practitioners about accessing social care research, from traditional material (such as books and journal articles) to online resources.

Taylor, B.J., Dempster, M. and Donnell, M. (2003) Hidden gems: systematically searching electronic databases for research publications for social work and social care. *British Journal of Social Work*, 33: 423–39.

This article discusses evidence-based practice in social work, systematic reviews, and accessing research relevant to social work.

Chapter 3: Appraising Research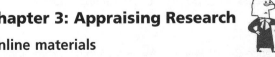

Online materials

Bandolier Bias Guide *www.jr2.ox.ac.uk/bandolier/Extraforbando/Bias.pdf*

A document that talks about bias in research.

Centre for Evidence-Based Social Services
                          www.cebss.org/appraising_research.html
An introduction to critical appraisal, including downloadable critical appraisal 'tools'.

Center for Social Research Methods   *www.socialresearchmethods.net/*
This website contains lots of information about types of research design, and includes research methods tutorials.

Critical Appraisal Skills Programme (CASP)   *www.phru.nhs.uk/casp/casp.htm*
This organisation was developed to build an evidence-based approach in to health and social care. It provides information about understanding research and offers training in this area.

Framework for Critically Appraising Research Articles
                          hsc.uwe.ac.uk/dataanalysis/crithome.htm
Provides advice about critical appraisal and contains a worked example.

How to Read a Paper   *bmj.bmjjournals.com/collections/read.shtml*
A series of papers from the British Medical Journal about critically appraising research. Subjects covered include: papers that go beyond numbers (qualitative research); papers that summarise other papers (systematic reviews and meta-analyses); papers that tell you what things cost (economic analyses); papers that report diagnostic or screening tests; papers that report drug trials; statistics for non-statisticians; assessing the methodological quality of published papers; getting your bearings (deciding what a paper is about); the Medline database.

Occupational Therapy Evidence-Based Practice Research Group
                          www-fhs.mcmaster.ca/rehab/ebp/
Provides tools for and advice on appraising research papers.

Research Design Explained
                          http://spsp.clarion.edu/mm/RDE3/start/default.html
Contains information about appraising research, as well as details regarding different types of quantitative study designs and about writing up research.

What is Critical Appraisal?
    www.evidence-based-medicine.co.uk/ebmfiles/WhatisCriticalAppraisal.pdf
A short document that discusses the purpose of critical appraisal.

Printed materials

Gibbs, L.E. (2003). *Evidence-Based Practice for the Helping Professions: A Practical Guide with Multimedia.* Pacific Grove, CA: Brooks/Cole.
Contains chapters on evaluating the quality of different types of studies.

Greenhalgh, T. (2000) *How to Read a Paper: A Guide to Evidence-Based Medicine*. 2nd edn, London: BMJ Publishing.

Although written for a medical audience, this book contains useful information for social care practitioners wishing to work their way through a piece of research.

Sheppard, M. (2004) *Appraising and Using Social Research in the Human Services: An Introduction for Social Work and Health Professionals*. London: Jessica Kingsley.

A basic introduction to research methods which offers useful advice on the advantages and disadvantages of different approaches.

Chapter 4: Understanding Statistics

Online materials

Introduction to Descriptive Statistics *www.mste.uiuc.edu/hill/dstat/dstat.html*

Provides information about basic statistical terms, such as averages (mean, median and mode) and standard deviation.

Statistics at Square One

http://bmj.bmjjournals.com/collections/statsbk/index.shtml

This resource contains a basic introduction for anyone wanting to find out about statistics.

The Really Easy Statistics Site

http://helios.bto.ed.ac.uk/bto/statistics/tress1.html

Contains information about some basic statistical terms, including details on calculating statistical data.

What is . . .? *www.evidence-based-medicine.co.uk/What_is_series.html*

A series of webpages explaining various statistical terms.

Printed materials

Best, J. (2001) *Damned Lies and Statistics: Untangling Numbers From the Media, Politicians and Activists*. London: University of California Press.

A guide to thinking critically about statistics referred to in the media.

Gonick, L. and Smith, W. (2000) *The Cartoon Guide to Statistics*. New York: Harper Collins.

This book takes a humorous approach to statistics. It begins with a brief history of the subject and then covers topics crucial to the study of statistics.

Greene, J. and D'Oliveria, M. (2001) *Learning to use Statistical Tests in Psychology.* 2nd edn, Buckingham: Open University Press.

Although aimed at psychology students, a useful handbook introducing the basic principles of experimental design and providing more in-depth information about when to use which statistical tests.

Kranzler, G.D. and Moursund, J.P. (1999) *Statistics for the Terrified.* 2nd edn, London: Prentice.

Introducing statistics for the social sciences, this book can refresh those who have undertaken statistics training, and can help those new to the subject to understand this topic.

Smeeton, N. and Goda, D. (2003) Conducting and presenting social work research: some basic statistical considerations. *British Journal of Social Work,* 33: 567–73.

A paper providing advice to social workers carrying out their own evaluations in relation to (a) conducting the project and (b) statistical analyses they may undertake.

Utts, J.M. (1999) *Seeing Through Statistics.* 2nd edn, CA: Duxbury Press.

This book looks at statistical methods from a 'real-life' perspective, with an emphasis on understanding rather than computing information.

Weinbach, R.W. and Grinnell, R.M. (2001) *Statistics for Social Workers.* Needhan Heights, MA: Allyn and Bacon.

No prior knowledge of statistics is assumed in this text, which offers a number of social work related examples to explain statistical analyses social workers are likely to encounter.

Chapter 5: User Involvement

Online materials

Best Treatments   *www.besttreatments.co.uk/btuk/home.html*

This site has a section for patients, which has information about different mental and physical conditions and about interventions that work, based on the best available research.

Cochrane Collaboration's Consumer Network *www.cochrane.org/consumers/*

A website that discusses the role of consumers in the Cochrane Collaboration. It provides information about Cochrane and its work, and about the opportunity for consumer involvement.

Consumers and Guidelines: How to Involve Consumers in the Development of Best-Practice Guidelines
www.enigma.co.nz/hcro/website/index.cfm?fuseaction=articledisplay&FeatureID=76

An article by Warren Lindberg about involving consumers in the production of guidelines.

Consumer Involvement in the Centre for Health Services Research
www.publichealth.gov.au/symposiumpdf/coghlan.pdf

An article exploring different models for involving consumers in health care decision making.

Guide to Producing Health Information
www.abdn.ac.uk/hsru/guide/orgs.shtml

This webpage is a useful resource for practitioners wishing to produce quality information materials for service users about interventions.

Has Service User Participation Made a Difference to Social Care Services?
www.scie.org.uk/publications/positionpapers/pp03.pdf

A position paper from the Social Care Institute for Excellence (SCIE) that looks at literature examining whether user participation has changed social care services.

How to Prepare and Present Evidence-Based Information for Consumers of Health Services   *www.health.gov.au/nhmrc/publications/pdf/cp72.pdf*

A review of literature focusing on the information needs of consumers and how to develop helpful material.

Informed Health Online *www.informedhealthonline.org/item.aspx?tabid=20*

Provides information and advice about how to help people keep up to date with reliable, evidence-based information.

INVOLVE   *www.invo.org.uk/index.htm*

This organisation aims to promote public involvement in health and social care research. Its website has information about the activities of INVOLVE and copies of its publications.

Involving Consumers in the Development and Evaluation of Health Information   *www.hfht.org/nhsdo/downloads/Topic_Bulletin4.pdf*

An online leaflet about involving consumers in producing good quality patient information.

Personal Experiences of Health and Illness   *www.dipex.org/*
On this website you will find personal testimonies from people who have a range of health problems. You can watch video clips, listen to audio recordings, or simply read through people's experiences.

Physicians' and Patients' Choices in Evidence-Based Practice
http://bmj.bmjjournals.com/cgi/reprint/324/7350/1350
An editorial from the British Medical Journal focused on the inclusion of service users in evidence-based decision making.

Printed materials

Chambers, R., Drinkwater, C. and Boath, E. (2003) *Involving Patients and the Public: How to do it Better* 2nd edn, Radcliffe Medical Press: Abingdon.
This book offers practical advice about involving lay people in service delivery and about structures and developments that have been established to assist with this process.

Coulter, A. (1997) Partnerships with patients: the pros and cons of shared clinical decision-making. *Journal of Health Service Research Policy*, 2 (2): 112–21.
An article examining the evidence for and against involving service users in decision making.

Domenighetti, G., Grilli, R. and Liberati, A. (1998) Promoting consumers' demand for evidence-based medicine. *International Journal of Technology Assessment in Health Care*, 14 (1): 97–105.
An article about promoting evidence-based practice through 'bottom-up' pressure from service users demanding that interventions provided are evidence-based.

Edwards, A. and Elwyn, G. (Eds.) (2001) *Evidence-based Patient Choice: Inevitable Or Impossible?* Oxford: Oxford University Press.
This book provides advice and examples about how to provide services that offer evidence-based patient choice. It also discusses modifications required in training and organisations if this approach to practice is to be realised.

Egan, M., Dubouloz, C., Von Zweck, C. and Vallerand, J. (1998) The Client-Centred Evidence-Based Practice of Occupational Therapy. *Canadian Journal of Occupational Therapy*, 65: 3, 136–43.
This article presents a framework for evidence-based practice within occupational therapy that integrates knowledge from the client and practitioner.

Kemshall, H. and Littlechild, R. (Eds.) (2000) *User Involvement and Participation in Social Care: Research Informing Practice.* London, Philadelphia: Jessica Kingsley Publishers.

A series of chapters exploring how to involve users in the planning and delivery of services and in research.

Service First (1999) *How to Consult Your Users: An Introductory Guide.* London: The Cabinet Office.

Material about consulting with service users, including information about conducting surveys and focus groups to gather consumer feedback.

The Mental Health Foundation (1999) *The DIY Guide to Survivor Research: Everything You Always Wanted to Know About Survivor-Led Research But Were Afraid to Ask.* London: Mental Health Foundation.

A document dedicated to supporting service user researchers in their role.

Chapter 6: Implementation

Online materials

Applying Research Evidence to Individual Patients
            http://bmj.bmjjournals.com/cgi/content/full/316/7145/1621

An article from the British Medical Journal about applying evidence to individuals.

Getting Evidence in to Practice   *www.york.ac.uk/inst/crd/ehc51.pdf*

An 'Effective Health Care' Bulletin that draws on research about how best to support the use of evidence within practice.

Getting to Grips with the Detail
            www.jr2.ox.ac.uk/bandolier/Extraforbando/BHC3.pdf

A document about adopting an evidence-based approach to practice (from a mainly medical perspective).

Improving the Use of Research in Social Care Practice
            www.scie.org.uk/publications/knowledgereviews/kr07.pdf

An online review from the Social Care Institute for Excellence that examines how research is used in social care and different ways of promoting the use of research within social care. It also discusses future directions to ensure research is used within social care practice.

Is Research Working for You? Self Assessment Tool
      www.whatworksforchildren.org.uk/docs/tools/SelfAssessmtWEB.pdf
An audit tool to help your organisation make better use of research by assessing where it is in relation to the skills, structures and resources needed to do so.

Linking Research and Practice
      www.jrf.org.uk/knowledge/findings/socialcare/910.asp
A Joseph Rowntree Foundation 'findings' briefing of a report which highlights obstacles to successful integration of research into practice, and suggests a range of strategies to assist successful dissemination and implementation of research findings.

REAL Evidence-Based Team Working   *www.rip.org.uk/teams*
A document providing advice about using evidence within a team to inform decision-making.

Research Mindedness in Social Work and Social Care
      www.resmind.swap.ac.uk/
An online learning resource supporting skills for evidence-based social work.

Research Utilisation *www.evidencenetwork.org/cgi-win/enet.exe/PUBS?RURU*

Contains abstracts and some full text of key discussion papers and systematic reviews on the topic of using research in practice/ policy. Link to the Research Unit for Research Unit, part of the Evidence Network.

Seeing the Wood for the Trees
      www.jr2.ox.ac.uk/bandolier/Extraforbando/BHC2.pdf
A document about changing an organisation's practice to ensure that it is evidence-based (from a mainly medical perspective).

What Goes Wrong When Implementing Evidence-Based Practice
      www.jr2.ox.ac.uk/bandolier/Extraforbando/BHC1.pdf
Talks about traps to avoid when trying to implant an evidence-based approach to practice.

What to Do With the Evidence *www.shef.ac.uk/uni/projects/wrp/sem12.html*
An article about getting research into practice.

Printed materials

Barratt, M. (2003) Organisational support for evidence-based practice within child and family social work: a collaborative study. *Child and Family Social Work*, 8: 143–50.

A report on a piece of research that involved a range of practitioners providing children and families services. It focuses on professionals' views of evidence-based practice.

Bero, L.A., Grilli, R., Grimshaw, J.M., Harvey, E., Oxman, A.D. and Thomson, M.A. (1998) Closing the gap between research and practice: an overview of systematic reviews of interventions to promote the implementation of research findings. *British Medical Journal*, 317, 465–68.

A systematic review of the literature exploring what works in terms of getting research into practice, mainly in healthcare settings.

Dawes, M., Davies, P., Gray, A., Mant, J., Seers, K., and Snowball, R. (2000) *Evidence-Based Practice: A Primer for Health Care Professionals*. London: Churchill Livingstone.

Chapter 17 outlines different models of change and methods for bringing about organisational change, as well as advice on monitoring practice outcomes. Chapter 18 sets out the importance of auditing or evaluating change.

Frost, S., Moseley, A., Tierney, S., Hutton, Ellis, A., Duffy, M., and Newman, T. (forthcoming). *The Evidence Guide: Using Research and Evaluation in Social Care and Allied Professions*. Barnardo's/Centre for Evidence-Based Social Services.

A resource aimed to equip practitioners with the skills to 'do' evidence-based social care. One module looks at issues of applying research to practice and creating an organisation which is supportive of research use. Comes with slides and trainers' notes. Can be used as a training pack or a self-directed learning resource.

Gira, E.C., Kessler, M.L. and Poertner, J. (2004) Influencing social workers to use research evidence in practice: lessons from medicine and the allied health professions. *Research on Social Work Practice*. 14 (2): 68–79.

An article examining what messages social care professionals can learn from research looking at influencing healthcare practitioners to use evidence to support their practice based decision making.

Hughes, M., McNeish, D., Newman, T., Roberts, H. and Sachdev, D. (2000) *What Works? Making Connections: Linking Research and Practice*. Barnardo's/Joseph Rowntree Foundation.

A review of relevant literature on different approaches to research dissemination which also looks at existing initiatives to disseminate research in the field of social care, and reports on focus groups and interviews with key stakeholders. Highlights obstacles to successful integration of research into practice, and suggests a range of strategies to assist successful dissemination and implementation of research findings.

Sheldon, B., Chilvers, R., Ellis, A., Moseley, A. and Tierney, S. (in press) A pre-post empirical study of obstacles to, and opportunities for, evidence-based practice in social care. In Bilson, A. (Ed.) *Evidence-Based Practice and Social Work: International Research and Policy Perspectives.* London: Whiting and Birch.

A pre-post survey involving 2, 315 practitioners, who formed a representative, stratified sample of professional grade social care staff working in the South West of England. The survey looked at practitioners' opinions and knowledge of evidence-based practice.

Tickle-Degnen, L. (1998) Using research evidence in planning treatment for the individual client. *Canadian Journal of Occupational Therapy,* 65 (3): 152–9.

A paper that discusses the retrieval and use of research when planning services for a particular client.

Walter, I., Nutley, S. and Davies, H. (2003) *Research Impact: A Cross Sector Literature Review.* Research Unit for Research Utilisation, University of St. Andrews.

A systematic review of research on strategies and approaches to increasing uptake of research amongst a range of service areas including Health, Education and Social Care.

Walter, I., Nutley, S., Percy-Smith, J., McNeish, D. and Frost, S. (2004) *Improving the Use of Research in Social Care Practice.* Knowledge Review 7. Social Care Institute for Excellence.

A 'knowledge review' which systematically reviews the literature on the use of research by social care staff and how the use of research can be promoted in social care practice. The review also includes data from interviews and fieldwork seminars.

Index